JULES AND JIM

a film by

François Truffaut

translated from the French
by Nicholas Fry

Simon and Schuster, New York

Stills by courtesy of l'Avant-Scène du Cinéma and
the British Film Institute.

Frontispiece: François Truffaut; Jeanne Moreau; Oscar Werner and
Henri Serre

Library of Congress Catalog Card Number: 68-27592

CONTENTS

CREDITS:

Adaptation and dialogue	François Truffaut and Jean Gruault after the novel by Henri-Pierre Roche (Editions Gallimard)
Directed by	François Truffaut
Produced by	Carrosse Films and S.E.D.I.F.
Photography by	Raoul Coutard
Assistant directors	Georges Pellegrin and Robert Bober
Edited by	Claudine Bouche
Music	Georges Delerue
Song	'Le Tourbillon'. Words and music by Bassiak
Colour	Black and white
Distributed by	Cinedis
Running time	1 hour 45 minutes
First shown	23rd January, 1962, at the Studio Publicis and at the Vendôme (Paris)

CAST:

Catherine	Jeanne Moreau
Jules	Oscar Werner
Jim	Henri Serre
Gilberte	Vanna Urbino
Albert	Boris Bassiak
Sabine	Sabine Haudepin
Thérèse	Marie Dubois
1st customer in the café	Jean-Louis Richard
2nd customer in the café	Michel Varesano
Drunkard in the café	Pierre Fabre
Albert's friend	Danielle Bassiak
Merlin	Bernard Largemains
Mathilde	Elen Bober
And the voice of	Michel Subor

JULES AND JIM

*The screen remains dark for a few seconds while a
woman's voice is heard.*

JEANNE MOREAU *off*: You said to me: I love you. I said to
you: wait. I was going to say: take me. You said to me: go
away.

*After these words, the screen lightens and the credits
come up against a series of fleeting images. Two men —*
JULES *and* JIM *— exchange elaborate greetings in a
narrow street, then are seen walking in a sunlit countryside with two girls. As the name* SABINE HAUDEPIN *passes
across the screen, a little girl is seen playing with a bow
and arrow. Close-up of the child's face. The camera then
pans rapidly towards the target, following an arrow.*

As the credits continue, JULES *and* JIM *are seen in various
poses: fighting a mock duel with broom handles instead
of swords; playing at the blind man and the cripple.* JULES,
as the cripple, is perched on the shoulders of JIM, *as the
blind man, who walks forward with his hands stretched
out in front of him. Then close-up of an hour-glass with
sand pouring through it; a Picasso of the Blue Period;
the guitarist Bassiak, who plays* ALBERT; JULES *walking
in a meadow with his daughter* SABINE, *holding her by
the hand. The final image behind the credits shows*
JULES *and* JIM *in the country, racing each other fran-
tically.*

*The credits end and the film opens with a series of
silent scenes between* JULES *and* JIM, *while a voice
describes the beginning of their friendship.* JULES *and*
JIM *are seated face to face at a table, playing dominoes.*

VOICE *off*: It was about 1912. Jules, a stranger to Paris . . .
Close-up of JULES, *the fair-haired one, moving a domino . . .*
had asked Jim . . . *Cut to close-up of* JIM, *the dark-haired*

11

one, looking at the game . . . whom he hardly knew, to get him into the Quatres Arts Ball. Jim had got him an invitation and had taken him to the outfitters. It was as Jules was rummaging in his gentle way among the materials . . . *Shot of* JULES *and* JIM *going through a large trunk: they take out a sheet* . . . choosing for himself a simple slave's costume, that the friendship of Jim for Jules was born. This feeling grew during the ball itself, where Jules looked on quietly, his large round eyes full of gentleness and good humour.

The next day . . . *Shot of the two men seated.* JIM *is cutting the pages of a book for* JULES . . . they had their first real conversation, then they saw each other every day. *Another shot of the two men. The camera follows them as they walk through the streets at night, deep in conversation.* They talked into the early hours of the morning, each teaching the other his own language and literature. They showed each other their poems and translated them together. They also shared a relative indifference towards money and they chatted easily, each finding in the other the best listener of his life. *Exterior shot of* JULES *and* JIM *in a moving boat with two girls;* JIM *is rowing.*

There were no women in Jules's life in Paris, and he wanted one. In Jim's life there were several. *Shot of* JULES *and* JIM *with two other girls near a summerhouse.* Jim introduced him to a young woman who was a musician. It seemed a good beginning. Jules was a little bit in love with her for a week, and she with him. *Shot of* JIM *smiling at a girl beside him, and pan to* JULES, *by himself, eating a cake.* Then there was a pretty, free and easy girl who stuck it out in the cafés until six in the morning, outlasting even the poets. Another time it was a pretty blonde widow, and the three of them went out together. *Shot of the courtyard of* JULES'S *apartment; a young woman comes out of a door. Zoom back to show her greeting first* JIM, *and then* JULES. She disconcerted Jules, whom she liked, but found a little dull . . . *Shot of the same girl with* JULES, *then pan to another girl* . . . and brought along a friend for him, a placid girl, but Jules found her too placid. Finally, against Jim's advice, Jules turned to the professionals . . .

Close-up of a hotel sign. JULES *approaches and goes inside. Shot through a window of a man kissing a woman's hand; then cut to a close-up of a leg, clad in a black stocking with a watch bracelet round the ankle* . . . but without satisfying himself there.

Cut to the narrow and badly-lit streets of Paris at night. The camera pans after JULES *and* JIM *as they walk along, deep in conversation. They pass a man and a girl,* MERLIN *and* THERESE, *who embrace each other passionately at the men's approach. As* JULES *and* JIM *move away,* MERLIN *draws back. The words* ' DEATH TO ' *have been daubed in great white letters on a hoarding behind them.*

MERLIN : Come on, to work !

MERLIN takes a brush from a bucket of paint held by THERESE *and daubs five more letters, so that the slogan reads* ' DEATH TO OTHER,' *but he finds that there is not enough paint left for the final* ' S.'

MERLIN *furious*: We've run out of paint, you little bitch ! *He hits her. (Still on page 2)* Now everyone'll think the anarchists can't spell.

Long shot of MERLIN *about to hit* THERESE *again; she escapes from him and runs towards the camera. She catches up with* JULES *and* JIM.

THERESE : Save me ! Merlin's after me. He's tougher than you are. Let's all run for it.

She pushes between the two men, taking them by the arm, and drags them off. Dissolve to the inside of a cab. THERESE *is sitting between* JULES *and* JIM *and the three of them are rather cramped. Shots of each of them in turn followed by a shot of all three.*

THERESE : Could you give me a bed for the night ? I'm Thérèse.

JIM : What, Thérèse? No, you really can't sleep at my place . . . I'm expected elsewhere.

JULES : Gilberte? *A pause, then* JULES, *rather shyly, turns to* THERESE. But at Jules's place . . . that's me.

13

THERESE *to* JIM : And who are you?

JIM : Jim.

THERESE : Jim and Jules, then.

JIM, *as if she had made a terrible blunder* : Oh no! Jules and Jim! *They laugh.*

> *Long shot of the cab moving off into the distance.*
>
> *Cut to outside* JULES'S *apartment; a door opens, and* THERESE *steps into the courtyard, followed by* JULES. *He shows her the stairway leading up to the apartment and they both go up.*
>
> *Inside the apartment, the door opens and the two of them come in. The camera pans after* JULES *as he searches for matches. Close-up of* THERESE'S *face, lit by the flare of a match off-screen. The camera moves rapidly to* JULES, *then cuts back to* THERESE, *who is smiling. Medium shot of* JULES *coming back towards* THERESE. *He picks up an enormous hour-glass and turns it over.*

THERESE : What's that?

JULES : It's better than a clock. When all the sand has run out, I must go to sleep.

> THERESE *fiddles thoughtfully with a device for rolling cigarettes. The camera pans after* JULES *as he comes in from the next room carrying a rocking chair.*

JULES, *showing her first the bed and then the chair* : You sleep here and I'll sleep there.

THERESE *with a touch of irony* : Yes, that's right. *A pause.* Have you got any cigarettes?

> JULES *steps hastily over to the bed and picks up a cigarette-box shaped like a domino, which he opens and holds out to* THERESE.

THERESE *looking up* : So you're Jim?

JULES : No, Jules.

THERESE *smiling* : You're nice, Jules.

> *She takes a cigarette from the box;* JULES *holds out his lighter.*

THERESE *lighting her cigarette* : I'll do my steam-engine act for you. (*Still on page 2*)

> *She puts the lighted end of the cigarette in her mouth*

14

and blows hard: smoke pours from the other end. Still puffing, she throws herself backwards onto the bed, then gets up. The camera pans after her in close-up as she puffs rapidly round the room, ending by the rocking-chair, where JULES *is sprawled, a little surprised. She kneels down beside him and puts the cigarette between his lips. Close-up of the two of them.*

The scene dissolves slowly to a long shot of GILBERTE'S *bedroom.* GILBERTE *is lying in bed, and* JIM *is sitting beside her with his back to the camera.*

JIM : In ten minutes it will be morning.

GILBERTE : Jim, just for once, you could stay here and sleep beside me.

> JIM *has got up to finish dressing. He buttons his waistcoat, then goes over to a mirror and smoothes down his moustache.*

JIM : No, Gilberte. If I stayed with you now, I would feel I was deserting you if I didn't stay tomorrow as well . . . and if I stayed tomorrow, we would be living together, as good as married . . . Isn't that against our conventions?

GILBERTE : How logical you are!

> JIM *goes to the window, raises the curtain and looks out at the weather. Then he comes back towards the bed, putting on his jacket and talking all the time.*

JIM : Also there is Judex, who doesn't like being left at home by himself . . . and anyway, the night is over, dawn is coming.

> *He sits again on the bed, kisses* GILBERTE, *(Still on page 3) then gets up.*

JIM : Look, imagine I'm a workman going off to the building site.

> *The camera pans after* JIM *as he goes out of the room and shuts the door.*

GILBERTE : Cad! . . . You'll go home and sleep until midday . . . I know! . . .

> *Outside it is dawn, and* JIM *is seen strolling down the street towards the apartment house where he lives. He passes several workmen, a cyclist, a cab, and as he arrives*

at the house and opens the door to go in, a late reveller crosses the street.

Dissolve to the interior of a café in the daytime. THERESE, JULES *and* JIM *have just come in and are looking for an empty table. The two men hang back, apparently engaged in a heated discussion.* THERESE, *slightly ahead of them, turns and points out a table.*

THERESE : Look, over there.

JULES *and* JIM *follow her, without paying her any attention, and sit down, still arguing.*

JULES : No, it was Shakespeare.

As the two men talk, THERESE *looks around and notices a man seated nearby;* * the man looks at her and gives a half-smile. (Still on page 4)* THERESE *turns to* JULES *and, after a moment, shakes him by the arm.*

THERESE *to* JULES : Jules, give me ten centimes, I want some music.

JULES *to* JIM : It was Shakespeare, I assure you.

JULES, *without turning round, takes some coins from his pocket and gives them to* THERESE.

JIM'S *reply is lost, as the camera follows* THERESE *across to the mechanical piano in one corner of the café. '* THE AZTEC' *also gets up and joins her.*

THERESE : Do you have a cigarette?

THE AZTEC : Yes, of course.

As he gives her a cigarette, the camera shows the two of them beside the mechanical piano. He lights a match for her. Cut to quick close-up of THERESE *doing her steam-engine act.*

THE AZTEC : I'm really keen on you.

THERESE *immediately takes him by the arm and leads him towards the door of the café. They go out and the camera pans after them from the inside of the café, as they go past the café window.*

THERESE : Could you give me a bed for tonight? I'm Thérèse.

---

* Purely for reference purposes, the man in question was jokingly christened 'The Aztec' in the original script.

The camera pans quickly back to JULES *and* JIM, *still seated at their table.* JULES, *sees the couple go, dumbfounded, and makes as if to go after them, but* JIM *holds him back.*

JIM : No, Jules . . . let her go . . . You lose one and find ten more.

JULES : I wasn't in love with Thérèse. For me, she was my young mother and my attentive daughter both at the same time.

The two men smoke. While JULES *continues to talk,* JIM, *who until now has been facing him across the table, moves round and settles himself beside* JULES *on the bench against the wall.*

JULES : I don't have any luck with Parisian women . . . Fortunately there are some girls back in Germany. I love one called Lucie. I asked her to marry me, but she refused. *As he talks,* JULES *takes out his wallet and produces two photographs: close-up of each of them.* I'll go back and see her. I gave myself six months. JIM *looks at the first photograph, then takes the second, which* JULES *is holding out to him.* There's another one : Birgitta . . . That's her. And another, Helga, I might perhaps love her if I didn't love Lucie. Look, this is her . . .

As he speaks, JULES *takes a piece of chalk from his pocket and draws a woman's face on the marble table-top in the style of Matisse. A shot shows his hand making the sketch. (Still on page 4)*

VOICE *off* : And, on the round table-top, Jules boldly sketched the face of a woman. Jim wanted to buy the table, but it was not possible . . . *Shot of the café from outside. Through the window,* JIM *is seen calling the proprietor and speaking to him in dumb show.* The proprietor was only willing to sell him all his twelve tables together.

Fade out.

JULES, *followed by* JIM, *passes through a very low doorway into the apartment of his friend* ALBERT, *who immediately comes to meet them with a young woman.*

17

JULES : Albert! . . . *Indicating* JIM . . . This is a French friend of mine.

THE WOMAN : Hallo. I think we have already met . . . *She pulls out chairs for them* . . . Please sit down.

VOICE *off* : Jim asked . . .

> JIM *turns to* JULES. *Shot of the two of them.*

JIM : Who is Albert?

JULES : A friend of painters and sculptors. He knows all those who will be famous in ten years' time.

> *The scene dissolves rapidly to another shot of the same room, in darkness except for a white, brilliantly-lit screen.* ALBERT *is standing beside a magic lantern, showing slides of various statues; in front of him,* JULES, JIM *and* THE WOMAN *are seated watching the screen.* ALBERT *gives a running commentary on the slides. (Still on page 21) Alternate shots of* ALBERT *and the screen.*

ALBERT : This one is more exotic; it looks rather like an Inca statue . . . *A pause* . . . This one is more Roman in style . . . It is badly weathered because I found it at the bottom of a garden. It must have been rained on for generations . . . *A pause* . . . Very pathetic, this one! The face looks positively decayed. It's very odd, too, to see the stone treated in such a flabby manner. *After another pause, a woman's head sculpted in stone appears on the screen: first in full-face, then in profile, then in detail; close-ups of the lips and eyes. She is very beautiful.* This one I like very much; the lips are very beautiful . . . a little disdainful. The eyes are very fine too.

> *There is a pause.* ALBERT *is about to change the slide when* JIM *turns round towards him. Shot of the three spectators.*

JIM : Could we see that one again, please?

ALBERT *nodding* : I have an even closer detail of it too.

> *Shots of the statue from different angles and in extreme close-up pass across the screen, dwelling in particular on the eyes and the mouth.*

VOICE *off* : The photographs showed a crudely sculptured woman's face wearing a tranquil smile which fascinated them . . .

18

Dissolve to an exterior shot on an island in the Adriatic. The two friends, wearing summer clothes, arrive at the top of a flight of steps overlooking a field full of statues. They descend and begin to inspect the figures.

VOICE *off* : The statue, recently excavated, was in an open-air museum on an island in the Adriatic. They decided to go and see it together, and set off immediately. They had both had similar light summer suits made for themselves. (*Still on page 21*)

The camera pans across the statues, finally coming to rest on the one already seen in the slides. Various shots of the statue, gleaming white in the sunlight.

VOICE *off* : They stayed by the statue for an hour. It exceeded all their expectations, and they walked rapidly round and round it, without saying a word. *Circular tracking shot round the statue.* Not until the following day did they talk about it . . . *Pause* . . . Had they ever met that smile before? Never!
. . . What would they do if they met it one day? They would follow it.

Period scenes of Paris: streets, the Métro, the Eiffel Tower.

VOICE *off* : Jules and Jim returned home, full of the revelation they had seen . . . and Paris took them gently back.

Long shot of the interior of a gymnasium. It is daytime. Various characters in vest and tights — the gymnastics costume of the period — are exercising either with batons or at French boxing, like JULES *and* JIM, *on whom the camera now closes. Shot of the two men boxing:* JIM *seems the stronger and more agile of the two. (Still on page 22) They finally stop to draw breath and retire to the side of the gymnasium, taking off their gloves.*

JULES : How is your book coming on?

JIM : I've done quite a lot of work on it . . . I think it will be . . . fairly . . . autobiographical; our friendship will play an important role in it. I would like to read you a passage of it.

JULES : Do please.

JIM *goes to get his manuscript; the camera holds on a*

thoughtful JULES. JIM *returns with the manuscript and reads to him.*

JIM *reading*: Jacques and Julien were constantly together. Julien's last novel had been a success. In it he described, in a fairy-tale atmosphere, the women he had known . . . before he knew Jacques and even before Lucienne. Jacques was proud for Julien. They came to be known as Don Quixote and Sancho Panza, and soon, unknown to them, their behaviour led to much rumour and speculation among the people of their neighbourhood. They ate together in small bistros. They smoked cigars extravagantly. Each chose only the best things for the other.

JULES *after a silence*: It's really very fine . . . If you will let me, I would like to translate it into German.

Looking pleased, JIM *nods agreement and takes his friend by the arm.*

JIM: And now for a shower!

Medium shot of two adjacent shower cubicles in the gymnasium. JIM *is in the left-hand one,* JULES *in the other. Standing under the showers, the two friends talk loudly to each other across the partition, raising their voices above the noise of the water.*

JULES: I've had a letter from my cousin. He says there are some girls arriving in Paris who were students with him in Munich. There's a girl from Berlin, one from Holland, and a French girl. They're coming to have dinner at my place tomorrow . . . *Louder* . . . I'm counting on you to be there.

As JULES *speaks, the camera moves towards him, then pans upwards. Close-up of the shower dissolving to a long shot of the courtyard outside* JULES'S *apartment.*

JULES *and* JIM *are seated at a table in the courtyard, talking. Three young women appear, coming down the flight of steps, and the two men jump to their feet and go to greet them. The third girl descends more slowly than her companions and, throwing back the veil of her hat, looks around her, taking in the scene and the two men. Close-up of her face: it bears a strange resemblance to that of the statue which so excited* JULES *and* JIM. *There*

20

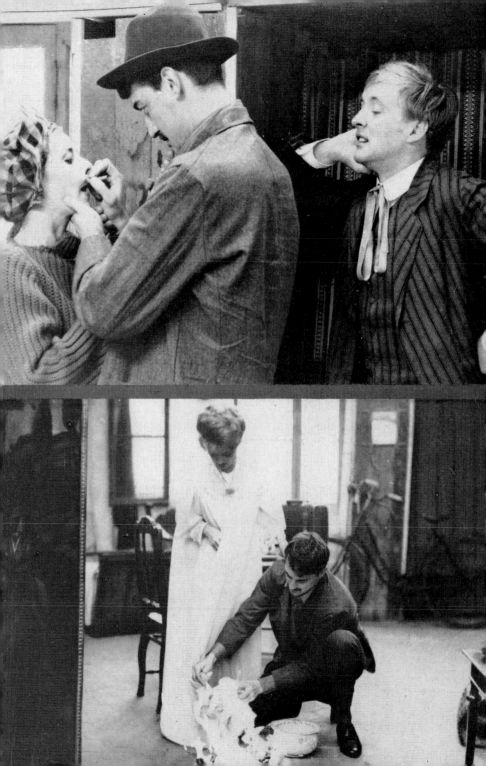

follows a series of close-ups of her eyes, mouth, nose, chin and forehead.

VOICE *off* : The French girl, Catherine, had the same smile as the statue on the island. Her nose, her mouth, her chin, her forehead, had the nobility of a certain province which she had once personified as a child in a religious festival. The occasion took on a dreamlike quality.

Dissolve to a shot of the same place a little later. JULES *is seen in close-up holding a glass. As he speaks, the camera tracks backwards to reveal the five people finishing dinner in the courtyard.*

JULES : Taking full advantage of my powers as organiser of this gathering, I propose that — in order to abolish once and for all such formalities as *Monsieur, Madame, Mademoiselle* and *My dear friend* — we drink our good health with my favourite Nussberger wine. We will avoid the traditional gesture of linking arms. The feet of all those present will touch under the table.

JULES *sits down. Group shot of the five of them seated round the table.*

VOICE *off* : Which was done.

Close-up of feet under the table: men's and women's shoes approach each other and touch.

VOICE *off* : In a state of high spirits, Jules quickly removed his feet . . . Jim's remained for a moment touching Catherine's, who gently removed hers first.

The camera pans up to the top of the table, framing the five people once more. JULES *looks at* CATHERINE *sitting beside him. They drink and laugh. The screen narrows to frame the pair of them, radiating happiness.*

VOICE *off* : A happy, timid smile appeared on Jules's lips, telling the others that they were in his heart.

Interior shot of a room in the gymnasium: JULES *and* JIM *are lying down side by side, taking a massage.* JULES *is reading the German translation he has made of* JIM'S *book. His voice fades rapidly, giving way to the* VOICE *off.*

VOICE *off* : For a month, Jules disappeared completely. He

25

saw Catherine alone, and for his own ends. But it was natural that the two friends should meet again at the gymnasium.

JULES : . . . Dann ist es wohl besser für diesen Mann, nicht zu heiraten.

JIM : Very good, Jules.

JULES *after a pause* : Come and see Catherine and me . . . would you like to?

JIM : Certainly!

It is day. JULES, *followed by his friend* JIM, *is seen climbing the staircase leading to* CATHERINE'S *apartment. The camera follows the two of them in medium close-up.*

JULES : I've talked a lot about you . . . Catherine is very eager to know you better, but . . . *After some moments,* JULES *turns and looks gravely at* JIM, *while the two men pause on the stairs. The camera is at* JIM'S *level and* JULES *is seen from below.* Not this one, Jim, eh?*

JIM *nods and they continue up the staircase.*

Dissolve to a shot of CATHERINE'S *bedroom.* CATHERINE, *shot from behind, sees* JULES *and* JIM *through the window, coming up the last few steps of the staircase and approaching her door. She goes towards the curtain which hangs across the doorway. The two men enter. Long shot of the room.* JULES *bends over and speaks in* CATHERINE'S *ear. She is still wearing a nightdress.*

CATHERINE : Good morning, *Monsieur* Jeem. (*Still on page 22*)

JULES *to* CATHERINE, *as she goes behind a screen to dress* : You must pronounce it Djim, with a ' d ' in front as in English. *We see* CATHERINE *behind the screen, pulling on a pair of men's trousers.* Jeem isn't like him at all.

The two men each take a chair and sit down, while CATHERINE *appears, dressed up like Charlie Chaplin's* THE KID. *The camera pans as she moves towards them.*

JULES *to* JIM : What do you think of our friend Thomas? Can we go out with him?

---

* A subtitle reads ' Not this one, Jim! ' Truffaut considered this subtitle necessary both to emphasise the importance of the phrase and also because of Jules's foreign accent.

The two men inspect CATHERINE, *who is holding up a mirror and looking at herself in it. She has put on a cloth cap which hides her hair.*

JIM : Not bad at all. A shade of a moustache, perhaps?

The two men get up and go towards her. CATHERINE *continues to look in the mirror as* JIM *takes her by the chin, and with his other hand draws a moustache on her upper lip. (Still on page 23)* CATHERINE *laughs.* JULES *looks at her lovingly and, as she hangs up the mirror,* JIM *gives her a small cigar and lights it for her.*

CATHERINE : And now to test the street.

Exterior shot of a Paris street in the daytime. With the cigar in her mouth, CATHERINE *walks along in front of* JULES *and* JIM. *She turns round for a moment and pulls the cap down over her eyes. In another street, the trio are seen walking along by a railway bridge enclosed in wire mesh, and passing an outdoor urinal. A man comes out of the urinal with an unlit cigarette in his mouth and approaches* CATHERINE, *who is still ahead of her companions.*

PASSER-BY : Excuse me, *Monsieur,* do you have a light?

Close-up of CATHERINE *as the man lights his cigarette from the end of her cigar.*

PASSER-BY : Thank you, *Monsieur.*

Rapid dissolve to the three friends going down a flight of steps leading to a footbridge across some railway lines.

VOICE *off* : Catherine was very pleased with the success of her disguise. Jules and Jim were moved, as if by a symbol which they did not understand.

CATHERINE *sits down at the bottom of the flight of steps and looks at the sky.* JIM *looks at her and then looks up with her.*

JIM : Either I'm dreaming, or it's starting to rain.

CATHERINE *and* JULES : Perhaps it's both.

CATHERINE : If it's raining, then let's go off to the seaside. *She gets up and looks at them.* We leave tomorrow.

CATHERINE *rejoins the two men and leads them towards the footbridge. She looks along it to the other end, then makes a suggestion.*

CATHERINE : The track looks just right . . . I suggest we have a race, to see who can get to the other end of the bridge first.

The two men immediately agree and imitate CATHERINE, *crouching down in a starting position.*

JULES : Ready now? One . . . two . . . CATHERINE *sprints away* . . . Oh! . . . Three.

The two men tear after CATHERINE, *who is a couple of yards in front of them. The three of them are seen running towards the camera, which then pans to follow* CATHERINE'S *face in close-up. We hear the noise of her panting. Finally, she collapses with a triumphant cry into a squat at the other end of the bridge. The two men arrive panting and squat beside her.*

JIM : Thomas, you cheated.

CATHERINE : But I won.

JULES : Thomas always wins. He speaks three languages and swims like a fish.

JIM : Can Thomas do a hand stand against a wall?

CATHERINE : You can teach him.

She gets up and replaces JIM'S *hat on his head, for she has taken it from him a few seconds earlier.*

CATHERINE : *Monsieur* Jim, will you come and help me take my luggage to the station tomorrow?

As she says this, she gets up and runs off. The two friends exchange glances, then also get up and hurry after her.

JIM : What a mixture Catherine is!

JULES : Her father was an aristocrat, her mother was lower-class. Her father came from an old Burgundian family, her mother was English. For this reason, she ignores the average, and she teaches those she is drawn to . . .

JIM : What does she teach?

JULES : Shakespeare!

The camera pans as the two men come down the steps from the bridge. CATHERINE *is waiting for them at the bottom.*

VOICE *off* : Jim thought of Catherine as belonging to Jules to such an extent that he did not attempt to form a clear picture of her. Her mouth had once again put on the tranquil smile which was natural to her and expressed all of her.

The following morning, CATHERINE *is seen tidying her bedroom, surrounded by pieces of luggage. She is wearing a nightdress.* JIM *enters.*

CATHERINE : Good morning. I'm almost ready . . . I have only got to slip on my dress.

JIM *prepares to collect the luggage, throwing his hat carelessly on the bed.* CATHERINE *starts.*

CATHERINE : Oh! The hat! . . . Never put a hat on a bed.

She moves the hat, while JIM *busies himself with the luggage and goes towards a bicycle which is leaning against the wall.*

JIM : Are we taking the bicycle? . . . and the suitcase?

He takes the bicycle and puts it near the outside door, while CATHERINE *takes a chamber pot full of letters and empties it onto the wooden floor. She crouches over the papers.*

JIM : What are you doing?

CATHERINE *contemplating the letters* : I am going to burn these lies.

JIM *has sat down on the bed close by her.*

CATHERINE : Give me a light.

JIM *gives her a box of matches. She sets fire to the letters with great solemnity, and without appearing in the least embarrassed by* JIM'S *presence. Rapid pan to the papers burning beside the chamber pot. The bottom of* CATHERINE'S *nightdress catches fire and she cries out.* JIM *jumps up, grabs a towel and wraps it round* CATHERINE'S *ankles. He then stamps out the burning papers. (Still on page 23)*

JIM : All right?

CATHERINE *takes refuge behind the screen.*

JIM : You haven't hurt yourself, I hope?

CATHERINE *off* : No, pass me my dress . . . There! . . . *she points* . . . at the foot of the bed.

JIM *fetches the dress and hands it to her, then examines the burnt papers.*

JIM : Have you got a broom?

CATHERINE *off* : Yes, right under your nose.

JIM sweeps up the papers and then piles the luggage all together by the door. CATHERINE comes out from behind the screen, fully dressed.

CATHERINE : Can you help me?

She turns round; he comes up to her and fastens the back of her dress.

JIM : There you are.

CATHERINE : Thank you.

CATHERINE looks at the luggage piled in the doorway, then looks round the room and picks up a small bottle from the table near her.

CATHERINE : We're taking this too.

JIM : What is it?

CATHERINE : Vitriol, to throw in the eyes of men who tell lies.

She starts to put the bottle in the last suitcase.

JIM : The bottle will break in the case. All your linen will get burnt . . . *A pause* . . . Besides, you can buy vitriol anywhere.

CATHERINE *in faked astonishment* : Really? . . . But it wouldn't be the same bottle . . . I swore I would only use this one.

Pan as CATHERINE goes across the room and empties the bottle down the sink, seen in close-up with smoke rising from it. Then resume on the centre of the room. JIM picks up the luggage. CATHERINE puts on her hat and gloves. As JIM now has his arms full of luggage she puts on his hat for him and they go out. Fade out.

Fade in to a shot of countryside in the South of France. The camera holds on the scene, as a train goes past, leaving a plume of smoke. Shot of sunlit coastal scenery. The camera tracks towards a white patch in the distance, which gradually turns into a handsome, white-painted house, standing by itself in the countryside.

VOICE *off* : They had to search for a long time before finding the house of their dreams to let. It was too large, but isolated, rather imposing, white inside and out, and unfurnished.

Low-angled shot of the house in medium close-up. The

30

shutters are closed. The façade is bathed in sunlight. Suddenly the centre window on the first floor opens and CATHERINE *appears on the balcony.*

CATHERINE *calling* : Jules!

Rapid pan to the next window, which opens to reveal a sleepy and tousled JULES.

CATHERINE : Did you sleep well?

JULES : Very well.

CATHERINE : Is Jim awake?

JULES : I don't know.

They look up at the floor above. The shutters of the central window open and JIM *appears, naked to the waist. He leans over the balcony and beams down at the others. (Still on page 24)*

JIM : How are the others?

JULES : The others are fine. *A pause.* What a beautiful day. . . . Come on, hurry up, we're going to the beach.

Slow dissolve: we are still near the house. The camera tracks forward to follow the three friends as they set out for a walk. At first they all hold hands like children . . . then they let go. They search the ground as they go, and now and then one of them picks up an unusual object— usually some piece of rubbish left by campers. They go towards a wood.

CATHERINE : Let's go in search of the last traces of civilisation . . . A piece of Hutchinson. *She shows her find to her friends, then throws it away.*

JIM : Look, a bottle.

JULES : A shoe.

Close-up of CATHERINE'S *hand picking up a piece of a plate.*

CATHERINE *off* : A piece of china.

Shot of the three of them, now inside the wood. CATHERINE *is in front.*

CATHERINE *looking from side to side* : Children, I rather think we're lost.

JULES *looking at a tree* : Then we must climb a tree.

Close-up of JIM'S *hands as he gives* JULES *a leg up the tree.* JULES *climbs up and looks around him. The camera pans across the tree-tops, as seen from* JULES'S *perch, and settles on a view of the house.*

JULES *calling out* : Yes, there's the house!

He comes down, and there follows a shot of the two men face to face, with CATHERINE *visible in the background, sitting at the foot of a tree. Medium close-up of* JULES *and* JIM.

JULES : Do you approve of my wanting to marry Catherine? *A pause.* Tell me quite frankly.

JIM : I wonder if she is really made for having a husband and children. I am afraid she will never be happy on this earth. She is an apparition for all to appreciate, perhaps, but not a woman for any one man.

Close-up of CATHERINE *sitting against the tree, then a long shot of the two men standing over her.*

JIM : We must move on.

CATHERINE : No, this time I won't move. I give up.

JULES and JIM : Come on . . . come on . . .

They pick her up, and, linking hands to form a chair, carry her off towards the house. Slow dissolve to a shot of CATHERINE, *on another day, running to the clothes-line in the garden of the house, on which three swimming costumes are drying. She takes them down.*

CATHERINE : Hey, boys . . . Come and help.

JULES *and* JIM *appear; she presents them with their costumes and they each take a bicycle and ride off. Group shot of the three of them riding along a road.* JIM *is in front, but* CATHERINE *soon catches him up.* JULES *pedals more slowly behind them. Series of different shots as they ride together to the beach: sometimes they are far apart, at other times they ride unhurriedly side by side; most often,* CATHERINE *races ahead while* JULES *and* JIM *pedal together.*

Dissolve to the beach. The two men emerge from the sea in swimming costumes and run laughing towards CATHERINE, *who is lying on the sand under a sunshade. Seeing them approach, she puts down the book she has*

32

been reading.

CATHERINE : At last! I have just read a book which I like. It's by a man, of course, a German, who dares to say out loud all the things I've thought quietly. The sky we can see is a hollow ball, no bigger than this . . . *She gestures to illustrate her theory* . . . We walk upright with our heads towards the centre . . . *Rapid shot of* JULES *gazing at her, while she speaks the following sentence in English* . . . The attraction pulls toward the outside under our feet toward that solid crust in which this bubble is enclosed.

Shot of JULES, *listening with interest, but concerned that* JIM *cannot understand. He translates for him, then gets up, satisfied. Group shot of the three of them.*

JIM : How thick is this crust? And what is there outside it?

CATHERINE : Go and see! What is there outside it! That's not the kind of question gentlemen should ask each other.

JIM also gets up and the two men run off down the beach, leaping in the air. Close-up of CATHERINE *watching them go.* JULES *and* JIM *are seen playing among the waves, then the camera resumes on* CATHERINE *who appears to have gone to sleep. (Still on page 24)*
Cut to a shot of the three friends, fully dressed, wheeling their bicycles up from the beach towards the road. CATHERINE *passes in front of the two men, who are walking side by side. Then* JULES *hurries ahead and catches her up. (Still on page 41)*

JULES : Catherine, give me your answer tomorrow. If it is no, I shall ask again every year on your birthday.

JULES and CATHERINE *pass on. The camera holds on* JIM, *who listens as* CATHERINE *speaks off.*

CATHERINE *off* : You haven't had much to do with women. . . . But I have known a lot of men. We'll cancel each other out, so perhaps we would make a good couple.

Long shot of the three of them mounting their bicycles and riding off. CATHERINE *speeds away in front, leaving* JULES *behind.* JIM *catches up with him and the two men pedal slowly side by side.*

JULES *to* JIM : I've asked Catherine to marry me. She has

more or less said yes.

The camera pans towards CATHERINE, *riding at full speed in front, and the scene slowly dissolves to a shot of a table in the garden outside the house. A hand moves a domino in close-up.*

CATHERINE *off*: When I was fifteen, I was in love with Napoleon.

Pan upwards to CATHERINE, *playing with a small bust of Napoleon. She is sitting on a bench, slightly to one side of the table, by the wall of the house. The two men are seated at the table, absorbed in a game of dominoes.*

CATHERINE: I dreamed that I met him in a lift. He made me pregnant and I never saw him again. Poor Napoleon . . . *She furtively embraces the statue. A pause: the two men continue their game without paying her any attention* . . . When I was a little girl they taught me 'Our Father which art in Heaven' and I thought it was 'Our father witch are in Heaven' . . . and I imagined my father on a broomstick casting spells before the gates of paradise . . . *A pause* . . . I have just told a story which was supposed to be funny . . . or in any case, amusing. You might at least laugh . . . Me, I can't even smile . . . *She shrugs furiously, then tries to scratch her back.* Would someone be so kind as to scratch my back for me?

JULES *absorbed in the game*: Heaven scratches those who scratch themselves.

CATHERINE: What?

She gets up and goes over to the table.

JULES *looking up*: Heaven scratches those . . .

He breaks off as CATHERINE *slaps him hard.*

CATHERINE: Take that! (*Still on page 41*)

He glares at her for a moment, then bursts out laughing. Pan to JIM *who also starts to laugh. Pan to* CATHERINE, *standing, who does likewise.*

CATHERINE *still laughing*: Before I knew you two, I never used to laugh. I used to look like this . . . *Series of close-ups of* CATHERINE *pulling faces, each new expression freezing for a moment* . . . or like this. That's all over; now I never look like

34

this . . . but like this ! . . . *They all laugh.*

Rapid dissolve to CATHERINE'S *window seen from the outside. It is raining. The window opens and* CATHERINE *appears on the balcony.*

CATHERINE : Is it raining? . . . Oh! Come and look.

The two men come out onto the balcony and JULES *puts his arm round* CATHERINE.

CATHERINE : I'm homesick for Paris, please let's go back to Paris. . . . We'll be in Paris tomorrow evening.

They go inside. Rapid fade out, then a series of low-angled shots of telegraph wires, followed by contemporary shots of the Gare de Lyon, the streets of Paris . . . and the courtyard of JULES'S *apartment.* JIM, *elegantly dressed and loaded with parcels, climbs the staircase to the apartment.*

In the next shot, he is seen arriving in the front room, which is empty. He puts down his parcels and claps his hands.

JIM *calling* : Catherine! . . .Jules!

They rush into the room full of congratulations.

JIM : It's all fixed. I've signed a contract with my publisher. *Picking up a parcel and presenting it to* CATHERINE. Here, this is for Catherine. *Then holding up a canvas by Picasso.* And this is for both of you.

JULES : It's splendid.

Having opened her parcel, CATHERINE *brandishes an elegant-looking back-scratcher.*

CATHERINE : What is it?

JIM : It's a little hand for scratching one's back with.

CATHERINE *tickles* JULES *with the back-scratcher and then tries it out on herself. Sobering up, they open the other parcels including a hatbox, from which they take two hats and put them on.*

JIM *off* : I'm taking you to the theatre. *Shot of the three of them.* I've got three seats for this evening.

CATHERINE : What are we going to see?

The camera follows JULES *as he fetches the hour-glass.*

JIM *off* : A new play by a Swedish author.

JULES : The theatre starts at nine o'clock. When the sand has run out, it will be time to dress.

The three friends go gaily out of the room and down into the courtyard, where they sit in a bower.

VOICE *off* : Jim saw his friends often. He enjoyed their company. The great Merovingian bed was officially inaugurated; Jules's two pillows now lay side by side and the bed was a good place. Catherine grew more and more beautiful as once again she learned to live.

Medium shot of a theatre balcony showing part of the audience. CATHERINE is seated between JULES and JIM. By a trick of the lighting, the shadow of the falling curtain can be seen on their faces. CATHERINE is applauding energetically, JIM less so. JULES is yawning.

Outside in the night, they are seen walking by the Seine. CATHERINE leads the two men down a flight of steps from the quayside to the river bank. It is very dark.

CATHERINE *taking off her jacket, and swinging it like a propeller* : All the same, the girl appeals to me. She wants to be free. She invents her life every moment.

JULES : Jim doesn't look enthralled.

JIM : Frankly I'm not. It is an obscure and deliberately sensational play. The author is another of these people who claim to show virtue better by depicting vice.

JULES : One doesn't know where or when it happens . . . The author doesn't explain whether the heroine is a virgin or not.

The three of them walk along the towpath as they continue their discussion. CATHERINE continues to swing her jacket.

CATHERINE : That's of no importance.

JIM : It would be of no importance if the conflict was a purely emotional one; but since the author makes a point of telling us that the hero is impotent, his brother a homosexual and his sister-in-law a nymphomaniac, he ought to give us some physical details about the heroine. It's only logical, don't you think?

CATHERINE : No . . . anyway, that's all you ever think about.

JULES : Exactly, *Madame,* that's all we ever think about, and you encourage us.

JIM : Let's not have any psychology this evening, Jules!

CATHERINE, *annoyed, goes on in front. A new shot shows her walking along beside the parapet above the water. She gets up onto the parapet and teeters along it, her jacket in her hand, holding out her arms to keep her .balance.*

JULES *off* : It's not a question of psychology, but of metaphysics. The most important factor in any relationship is the fidelity of the woman. The man's is of secondary importance. And who was it who wrote : ' Woman is natural, therefore abominable . . . ? '

JIM *off* : It was Baudelaire, but he was speaking of women of a particular class, of a particular society . . .

Cut back to the two men walking along the quay, oblivious of CATHERINE'S *antics on the parapet.*

JULES : Not at all. He was speaking of women in general. What he says of a young girl is magnificent : ' Horror, monster, assassin of art, little fool, little slut . . .' *The camera returns to* CATHERINE, *who has stopped for a moment, still ahead of the two men; she walks on, smiling, as* JULES *continues off* . . . ' The greatest imbecility coupled with the greatest depravation . . .' One moment, I haven't finished. And this is admirable . . . *Resume on* JULES *and* JIM *still talking, as they watch* CATHERINE *teetering dangerously along the parapet* . . . ' I have always been astonished that women are allowed in churches. What can they have to say to God? '

Pan to CATHERINE. *She turns back towards them.*

CATHERINE : You are a pair of idiots.

JIM : I personally haven't said a word, and I don't necessarily agree with everything Jules says at two o'clock in the morning.

CATHERINE, *in a quick close-up* : Then protest!

JIM *solemnly* : I protest.

At these words, CATHERINE *stretches out her arms (Still on page 42), drops her jacket on the ground, throws back her veil and jumps into the Seine.* JULES *and* JIM *rush to the parapet and look down at the water. All that can be seen is* CATHERINE'S *hat floating on the surface.*

Voice *off*: The sight of Catherine plunging into the river made such a strong impression on Jim that he did a drawing of it the next day . . . though he never normally drew. He felt a surge of admiration for her and mentally threw her a kiss. He was quite calm; he imagined himself swimming with her . . . holding his breath really to frighten Jules . . . On the surface, Catherine's hat drifted along with the current.

The two friends, having hurried down some steps, stand at the water's edge. Long shot across the water: CATHERINE'S *head reappears. She swims towards the steps, where* JULES *and* JIM *are standing, holding out their arms.*

JULES *and* JIM: Catherine! Catherine!

JULES: Catherine, you're crazy, quite crazy . . . *A pause* . . . Take my hand! . . . Here, Catherine! . . . here.

They haul her out of the water, and all three hurry into a taxi which is parked nearby.

Shot of the interior of the taxi. CATHERINE, *soaked to the skin, is seated between the two men.*

Voice *off*: Jules was pale, silent, looking less sure of himself than usual, and more handsome. Catherine wore the same smile as before, like a modest young general after his Italian campaign. They did not mention Catherine's leap into the river.

After going some distance, the taxi stops.

JIM: This is where I get out.

He begins to do so; but CATHERINE *holds him back.*

CATHERINE: Please, *Monsieur* Jim.

JIM: No, just Jim.

CATHERINE: Just Jim, I would like to have a talk with you and ask your advice. Will you meet me at seven o'clock tomorrow in the front room of our café?

JULES *to* JIM: Yes, Catherine wants to talk to you.

JIM: All right, I'll be there at seven o'clock.

He gets out and disappears into the night.

The next sequence opens with a long shot of the café interior. In the middle, facing the camera, JIM *is sitting at a table with a cigarette in his mouth. Rapid pan to the clock, which shows 7.15. The waiter serves several customers, who are seen in a series of shots: one, drunk, sitting by himself, is sprawled across the table next to a pile of saucers. Further on, two other customers are arguing. On the wall, a poster from an art gallery advertises a Picasso exhibition.*

A CUSTOMER : You're joking.

ANOTHER CUSTOMER : I never make jokes . . . moreover, I have no sense of humour. Of course, I know people who have got a sense of humour : friends of my wife, colleagues at the office ; but personally, I have no sense of humour.

After this sententious statement, the man puts his newspaper, Le Figaro, in his pocket and gets up. Cut back to JIM. During the commentary which follows, we see a series of shots of customers coming and going. (The images are masked on either side, making a narrower frame than usual.)

VOICE *off* : With his usual optimism, Jim had arrived late at the café. He was annoyed with himself, afraid that Catherine might have got there before him. He thought : ' A girl like her could quite well have come and gone, not finding me here at one minute past seven. A woman like her could have hurried across the café without seeing me behind my paper and gone off then and there.' He repeated to himself : ' A woman like her . . . A woman like her . . . But what is she like ? ' And for the first time, he began to think directly of Catherine.

The waiter moves from table to table, serving the customers. He is just behind JIM when, after a glance at the clock which shows 7.50, JIM calls him. (Still on page 42)

JIM : Waiter, another coffee please.

The customer, who is sprawled across the table, raises his head with difficulty.

THE DRUNKARD : Waiter, another glass.

The waiter returns and serves them. After a moment, JIM decides not to wait any longer. Close-up of him as he puts on his hat, gets up and goes out.

In another shot outside the café, CATHERINE, looking very elegant, comes nonchalantly towards the camera and looks in through the window. She goes in and comes out again, while a car passes noisily in the street. Her face registers acute disappointment. After a moment's hesitation, she goes away.

The shot dissolves rapidly to JIM'S *apartment at night.* JIM *is in bed, dozing. The telephone rings; he starts and picks up the receiver.*

JIM : Hallo.

Cut to JULES'S *apartment.* JULES *is lying in bed with* CATHERINE *by his side, talking into the telephone.*

JULES : Hallo, Jim! Did I wake you up? . . . Catherine and I are going back to my country . . . to get married.

CATHERINE leans quickly across and takes the second ear-piece from the telephone. She holds it to her ear and listens closely.

JIM'S *voice off, from the receiver*: Bravo, Jules! *Cut back to* JIM *in his apartment.* Please make my apologies to Catherine. I arrived late for our meeting . . . I waited until ten to eight.

Series of shots alternating from one apartment to the other, following the conversation.

JULES : She is more optimistic about time than you are. She was at the hairdresser's. She must have arrived at the café to have dinner with you at eight o'clock.

JIM : If I had imagined that she might still come, I would have waited until midnight.

JULES *off, from the receiver*: I'm passing you over to Catherine. She wants to speak to you.

CATHERINE has seized the receiver from JULES *and lies across him as she talks to* JIM, *while* JULES *takes the earpiece.* (Still on page 43)

CATHERINE : Hello, Jim. I'm very happy. Jules is going to teach me French boxing.

JIM *off, from the receiver*: French boxing with a slight Austrian accent.

CATHERINE smiles as JULES *takes the receiver back from her. As he speaks, he is gradually brought into close-up.*

JULES : Me? I haven't got an accent, my pronunciation is excellent. Let me show you. *In his heavy German accent, he*

40

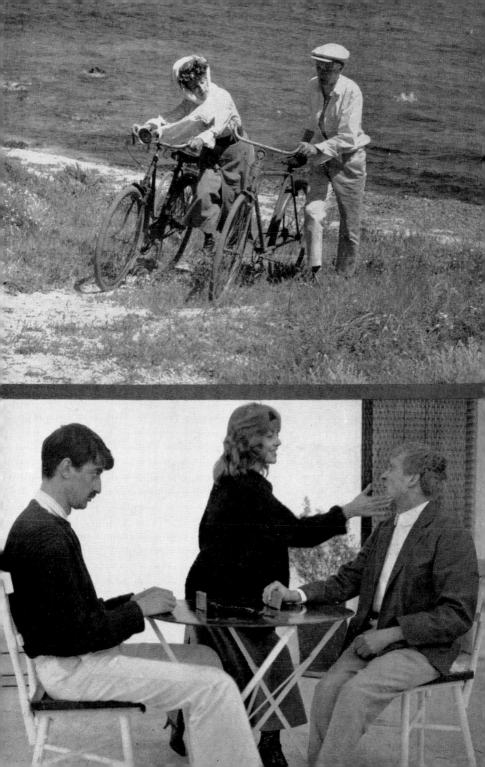

*starts to sing into the telephone, beating time with his free
hand. He seems very happy. (Still on page 43)*
JULES *singing*: Allons enfants de la Patrie,
            Le jour de gloire est arrivé.
            Contre nous de la tyrannie
            L'étendard sanglant est levé.
            A pause.
            Entendez-vous dans nos campagnes
            Mugir ces féroces soldats?
            Ils viennent jusque dans nos bras
            Egorger nos fils et nos compagnes.
JULES *sings louder and louder, with his accent getting
stronger and stronger, beating time energetically with his
hand.*
JULES *singing*: Aux armes, citoyens!
            Formez vos bataillons!
            Marchons, marchons,
            Qu'un sang impur
            Abreuve nos sillons.
            Nous entrerons dans la carrière . . .
*The song fades and the shot dissolves to a poster in close-
up bearing the words in French — GENERAL
MOBILISATION.**
*During the following commentary numerous newsreel
shots are shown (they are laterally distorted to give a
wide-screen effect): convoys of soldiers, a train leaving a
station, lorries, horses . . . a munitions train. Shot of
French soldiers marching, then of German soldiers doing
likewise. Shots of the trenches, where soldiers fight with
hand grenades and deafening noise. A shell bursts at the
entrance to a trench. Soldiers, both French and German,
fall. Cut back to the trenches. German soldiers attack a
trench with fixed bayonets, amid noises of bombs, shells,
and the chattering of machine-guns. Shots of soldiers*

* In the following sequences of the First World War, only the principal
shots are described in detail. Much of the material used is from
newsreel films taken at the time, which were lent to Truffaut by
the Service Cinématographique de l'Armée and Films de La Pléiade.

taken prisoner, some German, some French.

Voice *off*: Some days later, war broke out. Jules and Jim were mobilised, each in the army of his own country, and for a long time they had no news of each other.

Shot of trenches in the snow: a few soldiers, wrapped up against the snow, stamp their feet on the ground.

Voice *off*: The war seemed to be dragging on for ever and people began to get used to it. At the beginning, it was just a struggle which had to be fought, but little by little, an ordinary life had organised itself, following the rhythm of the seasons. A normal life with its slack periods, its routine, its pauses, and even its distractions.

More newsreel shots: a soldier buying a ticket at the box office of a ' theatre for the armed forces.' Close-up of a dancer, performing with exaggerated gestures on the stage. Long shot of the stage and the audience clapping. Other shots of trains, of soldiers on leave arriving at a station.

Voice *off*: Jim, in the trenches, received parcels from Gilberte. Several times, he told her that he was coming home on leave; several times, his leave was cancelled. Finally, in the spring of 1916, he came to spend a week in Paris.

Shot of an empty street in Paris, with a wooden hoarding on which are stuck numerous identical posters reading: NATIONAL DEFENCE LOAN. Medium close-up on one of these, then zoom backwards to frame Jim *in his trench coat and* Gilberte *walking arm in arm along the pavement. The camera pans after them. (Still on page 44)*

Gilberte: You don't marry a woman to thank her for sending you parcels . . . Things are fine as they are, I assure you.

Jim: As you wish. Even so, I have the feeling that we shall grow old together.

Gilberte: How is your friend Jules?

Jim: He married Catherine, but I haven't heard from him since . . . *A pause* . . . You know, Gilberte, sometimes in the trenches, I am afraid of killing Jules.

Cut to a battlefield. A bomb bursts in the foreground

46

with a loud explosion. There follows a series of shots of the German lines under bombardment. There is a deafening noise, clouds of smoke and dust. The camera moves along inside a trench. It tracks forward towards JULES, *who is sitting at a makeshift table, writing a letter by candle-light. He is in uniform; his pointed helmet rests on the table in front of him. He seems to read the letter over aloud.* (Still on page 44)*

JULES : Catherine, meine Geliebte, ich denke ununterbrocken an Dich, nicht an deine Seele, an die glaube ich nicht mehr, aber an deinen Korper, an deine Schenke, an deine Kuften. Ich denke auch an deinen Bauch und an unsern Sohn da innen. Ich habe keine Kuverts mehr und weiss darum nicht wie der diesen Brief senden soll. Ich werde an die Russische front geschickt; es wird schwer sein aber es ist mir lieber so, sonst würde ich in der standige Angst leben, Jim zu toten . . . Meine Geliebte, ich kusse deine Lippen wund.

JULES (*subtitles*) : My love, I think of you ceaselessly, not of your soul, for I no longer believe in it . . . but of your body, your thighs, your hips. I think of your belly, and of our son who is inside it. As I have no more envelopes, I don't know how to get this letter to you. I am going to be sent to the Russian front. It will be harder, but I prefer it, for otherwise I would live in constant fear of killing Jim. I kiss your lips passionately, my love.

A series of shell-bursts follows. Soldiers throw hand grenades and climb out of a trench. A section goes over the top to attack. Guns fire. Medium close-up of the trenches being hit by shells.

In the middle of a meadow, soldiers' hands, waving helmets, rise out of the tall grass . . .

VOICE *off* : Jules's country had lost the war, Jim's had won it. But the real victory was that they were alive . . . both of them . . .

Shots of a triumphal march-past in Paris, along the Champs Elysées; the Arc de Triomphe; joyous crowds on the boulevards.

---

* The voice is in German, a translation being provided by subtitles.

VOICE *off* : They communicated this fact to each other through a neutral country and resumed their correspondence as before.

JIM, in medium close-up, mounts a staircase. He looks rather tired and depressed.

VOICE *off* : Catherine and Jules were living in a chalet on the Rhine. A little girl, Sabine, had been born. Jim wrote to Jules : ' What do you think? Should I get married too? Should I have children? ' Jules replied : ' Come and see for yourself.'

Rapid shots in close-up of a photograph of JULES in uniform, and of JIM also in uniform.

VOICE *off* : Catherine added a few words inviting him, and Jim left. It was so important . . . that he took his time getting there.

In the next sequence JIM is seen walking along the hill-tops overlooking the Rhine. Long shot of the countryside, with JIM in medium close-up on the right. The camera pans, following his line of vision as he looks down on the scenery below.

VOICE *off* : Jim travelled slowly along the Rhine, stopping in several towns. An important Paris daily newspaper was publishing his articles on postwar Germany. He wanted to revisit the places where he had fought the hardest.

Various shots, mostly aerial views, of places in the countryside which JIM visits as if on a pilgrimage. In military cemeteries, JIM seems to search for the names of friends among the rows of white crosses.

VOICE *off* : In some places the bombardment had been so heavy that the ground was a mass of iron, and whole fields could not be cultivated.

Several shots in medium close-up of the war memorial at St. Armand.

VOICE *off* : These were turned into cemeteries, and Jim visited them, searching on the crosses for the names of comrades who had disappeared . . . cemeteries which already schoolchildren were brought to visit.

A small local train is seen from above (the sequence is shot from a helicopter). It is running through a wood and across open countryside towards a tiny country station. As it approaches the station, we see JIM *standing on the platform of the rear carriage, watching the passing scenery. Rapid cut to* CATHERINE *and her daughter, who is about six years old. They are behind the station barrier, watching the train come to a halt.*

VOICE *off* : Catherine was waiting for Jim at the exit of the little station with her daughter. Her eyes were dancing and alive with fantasy.

The train stops. As JIM *gets out, the camera pans rapidly after him. He shakes* CATHERINE'S *hand, then bends down to kiss* SABINE.

CATHERINE : Hallo, Jim . . . This is Sabine.

SABINE : Hallo, *Monsieur* Jim.

CATHERINE : Come on! . . . Jules is so keen to see you again.

JIM, *carrying his suitcase, follows* CATHERINE *and her daughter. Shot of the three of them from above, setting off down the road.*

VOICE *off* : Her low voice went with everything else. It seemed to Jim as though she had just arrived for their meeting at the café after a long delay, and that she had dressed specially for his benefit. She led Jim to their rustic chalet, standing surrounded by pine trees, close by a sloping meadow.

The camera tracks forward through the forest towards the chalet. JIM *has perched* SABINE *on his shoulders, and* CATHERINE *is walking beside them.*

In another shot, the chalet is seen coming closer and closer as they walk towards it. JULES *comes down the steps in front of the house and hurries towards* JIM. JIM *puts* SABINE *down and casually the two men embrace. There is a moment's silence; warmth and friendship flow between them.*

JULES : And how are the others?

JIM : The others . . . Oh! You know . . .

All four of them mount the steps to the terrace in front of the house. JULES *comes last, carrying* JIM'S *suitcase. The camera tracks sideways to follow them to the doorway.*

JULES : You haven't changed, Jim.

49

JIM : You haven't changed, Jules.

CATHERINE : In short, no one's changed.

Medium close-up of one of the windows of the chalet. Through the glass, we see the group coming in through the door. A clock is heard ticking. As they enter, long shot to show the living room. CATHERINE takes off her hat. JULES puts down the suitcase and sits in a rocking chair with SABINE on his knee, rocking gently. JIM sits near them, while CATHERINE goes to and fro, fetches glasses and puts them on the table. There follows a series of close-ups of each of them in turn, then a group shot. CATHERINE finally sits down and gives her daughter an apple, then offers JIM a drink.

JIM : No thanks.

CATHERINE *to* JULES : Do you want some?

JULES : Yes, just a little.

JIM offers a cigarette to CATHERINE, then to JULES.

CATHERINE : No thank you.

JULES : No thank you. I have stopped smoking since I learned to love nature.

There is an awkward silence. Close-ups of each of them in turn, then another shot of all three. (Still on page 61)

JULES : There's an angel passing by.

JIM takes out his watch and, after a pause, speaks.

JIM : It's quite normal. It's twenty past one. Angels always pass by at twenty past the hour.

JULES : I didn't know that.

CATHERINE : Neither did I.

Another silence.

JIM : At twenty past and also at twenty to.

Silence. Close-up of JULES and his daughter.

JULES *smiling* : So you won the war, you scoundrel.

Rapid pan ending in a close-up of JIM.

JIM *looking at JULES and his daughter* : Look, Jules, I would have preferred to win all this.

Rapid pan to JULES in close-up, giving SABINE a kiss.

CATHERINE *watches them and then gets up.*

CATHERINE : You must be hungry. Let's have lunch. Afterwards, I'll show you round the house.

They all move towards the table and take their places as directed by CATHERINE.

CATHERINE : Jim here, Jules there . . . and Sabine next to me. *While the two men embark on a conversation, the camera follows* CATHERINE *who has gone into the kitchen and is taking a soup tureen from the hands of the maid. She returns with it to the table.*

JULES *off* : What about your new novel?

JIM *off* : It's not finished yet, because of these blessed articles . . . I have to think about them all the week, then write through Friday night to airmail them on Saturday. What about you?

The camera cuts back to the two men. Close-up of JULES.

JULES : I've been commissioned to write a book on dragonflies. I am writing the text and fixing up the photographs. Catherine is doing the drawings and prints. Even Sabine helps . . . She comes to the swamps with me. *A pause.* I'm going to have an artificial swamp made in the garden.

Close-up of SABINE, *rubbing her eyes. Cut back to* JULES, *still in close-up, then successive close-ups of each person as they speak.*

JULES : Perhaps one day I shall return to literature with a novel about love — with insects for characters. I have a bad habit of over-specialisation. You spread your talents wide, Jim. I envy you.

JIM : Oh, me! I'm a failure. The little I know, I got from my teacher Albert Sorel. ' What do you want to be? ' he asked me — A diplomat — ' Have you got any money? ' — No — ' Is there some famous or illustrious name which you could, with some appearance of legality, add to your own? " — No — ' Then forget about diplomacy.' — But what shall I do then? — ' Look for curiosities.' — That's not an occupation — ' It's not an occupation *yet.* Travel, write, translate . . . learn to live anywhere. Start now, the future is bright for professional tourists. The French have spent too long cooped up behind their own frontiers. You will always find some newspaper to pay for your jaunts.'

Close-up of JULES, *who turns towards* CATHERINE. *The camera pans rapidly across and comes to rest on her, also in close-up.*

CATHERINE: Jules thinks you have a great career ahead of you. So do I, though I don't say it will necessarily be spectacular.

Cut to JULES'S *bedroom. The camera pans right round the room and comes to rest on* JIM *and* CATHERINE.

CATHERINE: This is where Jules works and sleeps. Our life is organised like a monastery's. Jules writes his books, chases after his insects and all kinds of other little creatures. Mathilde, whom you've seen, is the daughter of a neighbouring farmer. She helps us with the housework and with looking after Sabine.

In the next shot, CATHERINE *and* JIM *are on the landing.* CATHERINE *opens a door.*

CATHERINE: My bedroom.

Cut to JIM *and* CATHERINE *standing in the middle of* CATHERINE'S *room.* JIM *looks around him, and his eye is caught by a photograph pinned to the wall. Rapid insert of the photograph in close-up; it shows a young man wearing a wig and looking strangely like Mozart.*

JIM: But it's Jules!

CATHERINE: Yes . . . Jules's father was so fond of Mozart that one day he dressed Jules up as Mozart.

CATHERINE *smiles affectionately and leads* JIM *out onto the balcony. Rapid long-shot of the chalet from the exterior.*

CATHERINE: This is the balcony.

Cut back to the two of them. CATHERINE *points with her finger; the camera tracks across the countryside, following her line of vision.*

CATHERINE *off*: Down there is the inn where you will sleep tonight. Jules will take you there later on.

After a shot of the balcony from below, the camera pans downwards to show SABINE *and* JULES *playing horses; she is trotting behind him, while he pretends to be the*

*horse. They trot round in a circle on the terrace in front
of the house. At that moment,* Catherine *and* Jim
emerge from the chalet and come towards them. Jim
picks up Sabine *and throws her to* Jules, *who in turn
throws her to* Catherine. *All four of them then set off
gaily down towards the meadow. As we watch them go,*
Sabine *stumbles and falls down.* Jim *rushes forward to
pick her up . . . They walk on. The next shot shows
them in the meadow.* Jim *is carrying* Sabine *on his
shoulders; both of them are seen in close-up. He lays
her down on the ground and puts his arms around her,
and together they roll down the grassy slope, laughing
hilariously. Long shot of the house . . . We see the four
of them again walking in the country. The scene dissolves slowly to a shot of the table on the terrace, where*
Jules *and* Jim *are seated, playing dominoes.*

Voice *off* : Jules and Jim resumed their great conversation
which had been interrupted by the war. They recounted to
each other their experiences in the war . . . *A pause* . . . Jules
avoided talking about his family life. Catherine treated him
with a mixture of kindness and severity, but Jim had the
impression that all was not going well.

*The camera pans away from the table where the two
men are playing to show* Catherine *knitting with* Sabine
*at her side. (Still on page 61) It then tracks backwards
to reveal the two men again in the foreground. After a
while,* Catherine *stops knitting, leans towards* Sabine
and gives her a kiss in a rapid close-up.

Catherine : Time for bed, sailor, the fleas are hungry. *She
picks up the child.* There was once a flea, a nice little flea.
Turning towards Jim. Good night, Jim. Till tomorrow morning.

*We now see the four of them on the landing at the top
of the stairs.* Catherine, *who has* Sabine *perched on her
shoulder, goes into her room and shuts the door. The
camera holds on* Jules, *who takes* Jim *by the shoulder
and shows him the other door.*

Jules : I want to talk to you.

The two men enter JULES'S *bedroom-study. Medium close-up of the two of them.*

JULES : How do you find Catherine?

JIM : Marriage and motherhood seem to suit her. She seems a little less like the grasshopper . . . a little more like the ant.

JULES : Don't you believe it . . . She brings order and harmony to this house, certainly . . . But when things go too well, she begins to feel discontented. Her manner changes and she only says or does anything to lash out at everything.

JIM : I've always thought as much. Napoleon was the same.

JULES : She claims that the world is rich, that one can cheat a little from time to time, and she begs the good Lord's forgiveness for it in advance, sure that she will be granted it . . . JULES *gets up*. Jim, I'm afraid she may leave us.

JIM *astonished, in close-up* : It's not possible.

Close-up of JULES *sitting down again.*

JULES : Not at all . . . She already has once, for six months. I thought she would never come back. I can feel that she's on the point of leaving again. You know, Jim . . . she is no longer altogether my wife. She has had lovers. Three that I know of. One, on the eve of our wedding . . . as a gesture of farewell to her bachelor life ! . . . and in revenge for something I did, I don't know what . . . *The camera tracks backwards to show the two men together again.* I am not the man she needs, and she is not the kind of woman to put up with it. For myself, I have got used to the idea of her being unfaithful to me from time to time . . . but I couldn't bear her going away.

JULES *gets up and goes towards the window.* JIM, *completely taken aback and embarrassed by what he has just heard, follows him mechanically.*

JULES : Then there's Albert.

JIM : Ah yes, the singer who discovered the statue?

JULES : That's right. If you remember, it was through him that we got to know her.

In the following shot of the chalet at night, JULES *and* JIM *are seen from the outside, leaning on the window sill.*

JULES : He was wounded in the war. He is convalescing in a neighbouring village. Catherine has encouraged him, given

54

him some hope. He is a professional man . . . He talked to me quite freely. He wants to marry her and take the girl as well. I don't blame her. I don't blame her or Albert. I am gradually renouncing my claim to her, to everything I have wanted on this earth.

The camera pans very slowly across the forest.

JIM *off* : She won't leave you, because that is what she loves in you — the side of you which is like a Buddhist monk.

JULES : Normally she is sweet and kind, but if she feels that she is not being sufficiently appreciated, she becomes terrifying. She passes suddenly and violently from one extreme to the other. *A pause.* Listen to the song of that cricket; it is a kind of mole . . .

Fade out.

The camera iris opens gradually on a shot of wooded countryside. The chalet can be seen in the distance. As the shutter opens further, it reveals the embrasure of a window, and finally the face of JIM, *faintly visible behind the glass.*

VOICE *off* : From his room in the inn, Jim could see the chalet. So there was Catherine, the radiant queen of the household, ready to take flight at any moment. Jim was not surprised. He remembered Jules's mistakes with Thérèse, with Lucie, with all the others. *We move to the interior of* JIM'S *room in the inn:* JIM *goes over to the bed, empties his pockets, puts their contents on the bedside table and starts to undress.* He knew that Catherine was terribly demanding. Jim was filled with sadness for Jules, but he felt unable to condemn Catherine. She could have jumped at other men like she once jumped into the Seine . . . A threat seemed to be hanging over the household. *A pause.* A second week began.

Fade out.

It is evening. In the living room of the chalet, we see JIM *and* CATHERINE, *both reading.* JULES *is sitting in his rocking chair with* SABINE *on his knee. Medium close-up of* CATHERINE, *who looks up, takes off her glasses and rubs the bridge of her nose.*

CATHERINE : Sabine, I think it's time you said good night.

Pan as SABINE *takes hold of her mother's spectacles and puts them on.*

Close-up of SABINE *as she looks from side to side, then takes off the glasses and rubs the bridge of her nose, imitating her mother.*

SABINE : Yes, mummy.

She gets down from her father's knee and goes over to JIM *and kisses him.*

SABINE : Good night, Jim.

In the next shot, CATHERINE *is seen walking towards the door with* SABINE *in her arms. She hesitates and turns round.*

CATHERINE : Jim, I need to speak to you a little later. Will you be free?

Close-up of JIM *as he shoots a questioning glance at* JULES.

The camera switches rapidly to JULES, *also in close-up, as he replies with a look of acquiescence.* JIM *turns again towards* CATHERINE.

JIM : Of course.

CATHERINE *and her daughter go out of the room. Rapid shot, slightly from above, of* CATHERINE *going upstairs.*

CATHERINE : Mathilde, come with me.

Return to JULES *and* JIM *in the living room.* JULES *is still seated in his rocking chair with* JIM *close by.*

JULES : You will note that words cannot have the same significance in two different languages as they don't have the same gender. In German, war, death, the moon, are all masculine, while the sun and love are feminine. Life is neuter.

JIM : Life? Neuter? That's a nice concept, and very logical too.

Shot of CATHERINE *shutting her bedroom door and coming slowly down the stairs, listening to* JIM's *voice.*

JIM *off* : It was the same in France. The longer the war lasted, the shorter women's skirts became. Each time the soldiers came home on leave, there were rows. They thought their wives were making fools of them.

CATHERINE *comes into the living room, shuts the door*

56

and sits down.

JIM : The real reason was that cloth was becoming more and more scarce.

CATHERINE : It's like in the towns, where the women cut their hair so that they could work in the factories, among the machines and driving belts.

JULES : By the way, Jim, it's time you learned to appreciate German beer.

CATHERINE : Jim is like me, he's French, and he doesn't give a damn about German beer.

JIM : Not at all.

CATHERINE : What? But France has one of the greatest varieties of wines in Europe, in the whole world even. There's, oh I don't know, the Bordeaux wines : Château-Lafitte, Château-Margaux, Château-Yquem, Château-Frontenac, Saint-Emilien, Saint-Julien, Entre-deux-Mers, and I don't know what else even better. Then there's . . . wait a moment . . . Clos-Vougeot, the Burgundies : Romanée, Chambertin, Beaune, Pommard, Chablis, Montrachet, Volnay, and then the Beaujolais : Pouilly-Fuissé, Pouilly-Loché, Moulin-à-Vent, Fleurie, Morgon, Brouilly, Saint-Amour . . .

JULES : Our eyes are all riveted on the mortar bomb which is slowly coming down the stairs : only three more steps, only two more, everyone flat on their faces.

CATHERINE *gets up and makes for the door, then turns towards* JIM.

CATHERINE *quietly to* JIM : Catch me up !

She opens the door and runs out. JIM *gets up and rushes after her.*

Outside the chalet, it is dark. CATHERINE *has run out of the house and is seen disappearing into the forest, followed by* JIM. *Finally he catches her up and she leans against a tree, out of breath.*

CATHERINE : What do you want to know?

JIM : Nothing, I want to listen to *you.*

CATHERINE : To judge me?

JIM : God forbid.

CATHERINE : I don't want to say anything, I want to question

57

you. My question is, tell me about yourself, Jim.

JIM : All right, but what?

CATHERINE : It doesn't matter. Just talk away.

They walk off, the camera tracking sideways to follow them in medium close-up. CATHERINE *is once more slightly in front of* JIM.

VOICE *off* : Jim began : ' There were once two young men . . .' and he described, without mentioning their names, Jules and himself, their friendship, their life in Paris before the arrival of a certain young woman; how she came into their lives, like an apparition, and what happened afterwards. He even mentioned Jules's warning: ' *Not this one, Jim!* ' — Here Jim could not avoid mentioning his own name . . . how the three of them went out together, their holiday beside the sea. Catherine could see that Jim remembered everything which concerned her as clearly as if it had just happened. She disputed one or two details as a matter of principle, and added others. Jim described the time they had missed each other at the café. He talked to her about the three of them as he saw them, about Jules's hidden qualities, and told her how he had felt from the beginning that Jules would not be able to keep Catherine.

CATHERINE : Would you have told me all this at the café?

JIM : Yes.

CATHERINE : Go on.

JIM : There's no more to say. There was the war, my joy at finding Jules again, your appearance at the station, the happiness of these last few days I have spent near you, what I have seen, what I have learned, what I have guessed, this cloud on the horizon . . . I am referring to Albert.

CATHERINE : Are you with Jules against me?

JIM : No more than he is himself.

CATHERINE : I will start the story again from the beginning, as I have lived it myself. It was Jules's generosity, his innocence, his vulnerability which dazzled me, conquered me. He was so different from other men. By giving him happiness, I hoped to cure him of these crises where he felt lost and out of his depth. But I realised that these crises are an inseparable part of him. Our happiness, for we were happy, did not last, and there we were, face to face, linked together. His family was sheer purgatory for me. On the eve of our wedding, during a reception, Jules's mother wounded me deeply by her clumsy behaviour. Jules remained passive — which was tantamount to condoning it. I punished him immediately by taking up with an old lover, Harold . . . *Yes, lover.* That way I would be quits with Jules, when we were married; we could start again from scratch. Fortunately, the family has gone to live in the north, I don't know where. War broke out; Jules went off east. *They stop walking. Shot of* JIM, *who comes up to* CATHERINE. *Her voice continues off.* He wrote me marvellous, passionate love-letters. I loved him more at a distance. Once again, I saw him with a halo. Our final misunderstanding, the real rupture, came on his first leave. I felt I was in the arms of a stranger.

Medium shot of the two of them.

CATHERINE : He went off again. Sabine was born nine months later. *They resume walking.*

JIM : She doesn't look very like Jules.

JIM *has suddenly stopped and is looking at* CATHERINE.

CATHERINE : You can think what you like . . . she is his.

CATHERINE *continues walking. The camera tracks forwards, following the back of her neck as seen by* JIM.

CATHERINE : But I said to him : ' I have given you a daughter; that is enough for me. This chapter is closed. Let's sleep in separate rooms . . . I am taking back my liberty.' *A pause.* Do you remember our young friend, Fortunio? *She turns round and comes back towards* JIM. He was there, as free as air . . . and so was I. He was kind, he made a good partner. What a holiday we had! But he was too young; it wasn't a serious affair. And one fine day, to my surprise . . . *Close-up of* CATHERINE . . . I found I missed Jules's indulgent and leisurely ways. I felt drawn back to my daughter like a magnet. I was on the wrong track. So I left. I have only been back here three months.

Return to the two of them, seen from behind. CATHERINE *has taken* JIM'S *arm, and they walk on, arm in arm.*

CATHERINE : Jules is finished for me as a husband. Don't be sorry for him. I still allow him the distractions he needs . . . Then there is Albert. He has told me about the statue which the three of you fell in love with, and which I apparently look like. I've flirted with him. There are some bizarre sides to his character, but he has the natural authority which Jules lacks. He wants me to leave everything, to marry him. He would take the mother and daughter together. *In reverse shot, they are seen walking towards the camera.* I like him a lot, but nothing more — so far. Anyway, he is coming to lunch tomorrow. I shall see. You've been a good listener, I have talked more than you. I don't claim to have said everything, no more than you just now. Perhaps I have had other lovers; that's my affair. I have only talked about things which you mentioned yourself.

JIM : I understand you, Catherine.

CATHERINE : I don't want to be understood . . . *Raising her head slightly* . . . It's almost dawn now.

They have arrived at the bottom of the steps which lead up to the door of the chalet. CATHERINE *holds out her hand to* JIM, *who tries to draw her to him, but she disengages herself and goes up the steps. The camera holds on* JIM *as he watches her go without moving.*

VOICE *off* : Jim wanted Catherine, but he fought back the desire more than ever. She must not leave . . . How much did he want this for himself? He would never know. She was perhaps — Jim was by no means sure of it — deliberately seducing him. It was intangible. CATHERINE *stops at the door of the chalet and turns round.* JIM *runs off towards the inn.* Catherine only revealed the things she wanted when she had them in her hand.

Fade out.

The next sequence opens with a shot of ALBERT, *wheeling his bicycle along the path through the meadows leading to the chalet. He has a guitar slung across his back, and on catching sight of* SABINE, *he hurries towards her and kneels down to give her a hug. A few yards away,* JULES *and* JIM *are seated in the grass.*

60

ALBERT: Hallo, Sabine.
SABINE: Hallo, Albert.
ALBERT: How are things? How is your mummy?
SABINE: Well.

Long shot from above of JULES *and* JIM. *They are seen in medium close-up as* ALBERT *approaches and sits down beside them.*

JULES: Hallo, Albert.
JIM: I see you got rid of your moustache, too.
ALBERT: Oh yes. I did the same as everyone else. But I don't like myself without one — I feel naked. I'm going to let it grow again.
JULES: Albert was wounded during the war, in the trenches.
ALBERT: I'm quite all right now . . . but when I woke up and saw the surgeon poking around inside my skull, I thought of Oscar Wilde: 'My God, spare me the ills of the flesh; I will answer for the ills of the soul.'
JULES: The revolting thing about war is that it deprives a man of his own individual struggle.
JIM: Yes, that's true, but I think that he can still carry it on outside the field of war. I am thinking of a gunner I knew at the hospital. He was coming back from leave when he met a young girl on the train. They talked to each other all the way from Nice to Marseilles. As she stepped out onto the platform, she gave him her address. Then, for two years he wrote to her frenetically every day from the trenches, on bits of wrapping paper, by candle-light. He kept on writing even when the mortar bombs were raining down around him, and his letters became more and more intimate in tone. At first he began 'Dear Mademoiselle,' and ended 'With all good wishes.' In the third letter, he called her 'My little sylph,' and asked her for a photograph . . . Then it was 'My adorable sylph,' then 'I kiss your hands,' then 'I kiss your forehead.' Later on, he described the photograph she had sent him and talked about her bosom, which he thought he could see under her *peignoir*, and soon he dropped the formal mode of address and started to call her 'tu': 'Je t'aime terriblement.' One day, he wrote to the girl's mother asking for her hand and

became officially engaged to her, although he hardly knew her. The war went on and the letters became more and more intimate. ' I take hold of you, my love, I take your adorable breasts . . . I press you against me quite naked . . .' When she replied rather coldly to one of his letters, he flew into a passion and begged her . . . not to flirt with him because he might die from one day to the next. And he was right. *A pause.* You see, Jules, to understand this extraordinary deflowering by correspondence, one must have experienced all the violence of the war in the trenches, its particular kind of collective madness, with death constantly present. So there was a man who, at the same time as taking part in the Great War, managed to conduct his own little parallel war, his individual struggle, and completely conquer the heart of a woman from a distance.

When he arrived at the hospital, he was wounded in the head like you, but he wasn't as lucky as you. He died after being trepanned, just the day before the armistice. In his last letter to the fiancée he hardly knew, he wrote : ' Your breasts are the only bombs I love.' I'll show you a series of photographs I have of him . . . If one looks at them quickly, one has the illusion that he is moving.

Medium shot of CATHERINE *at the window, leaning her head on her hand.*

CATHERINE : It's a beautiful story . . . When he was away fighting, Jules sent me some very beautiful letters too.

Medium close-up of the three men.

CATHERINE *off* : Hello, Albert . . . Have you finished my song? . . . Come on up, and we'll work on it together.

ALBERT *gets up and walks towards the house, leaving behind his guitar.* SABINE *runs after him with it.*

SABINE : Albert, Albert, Albert . . .

ALBERT *turns round, takes the guitar and goes up the steps to the house. He goes up to* CATHERINE, *who is waiting for him at the door, and kisses her.*

Long shot of the living room with ALBERT, *sitting in the rocking chair,* CATHERINE, *sitting on a stool,* JULES *and* JIM.

ALBERT : The rocking of this chair is an invitation to the pleasures of the flesh.

JULES : What about this song?

ALBERT : We've nearly got it right now.

CATHERINE : Yes, we have, haven't we, Albert? . . . Shall we start?

ALBERT *gets up to fetch his guitar and* JULES *takes his place in the rocking chair.* ALBERT *sits at* CATHERINE'S *feet.*

CATHERINE : In my opinion, it's much too good for them, but never mind, one can't be choosy about one's audience!

There follows the song 'Le Tourbillon' ('The Whirlwind'). *Long shot of the living room.*

Elle avait des bagues à chaque doigt,
Des tas de bracelets autour des poignets,
Et puis elle chantait avec une voix
Qui, sitôt, m'enjola.
(On every finger she wore rings
Round her wrists, bracelets and things,
And when she sang, her voice made me
Lose my head, you see.)

Medium shot of ALBERT *accompanying* CATHERINE *on the guitar as she sings* (*Still on page 62*)

Elle avait des yeux, des yeux d'opale,
Qui me fascinaient, qui me fascinaient.
Y avait l'opale de son visage pâle
De femme fatale qui m'fut fatale (twice).
(Her eyes were like two opals bright
That gave me a chill, gave me a thrill,
Her face was like an opal white
As she moved in for the kill.)

Close-up of ALBERT.

On s'est connu, on s'est reconnu
On s'est perdu de vue, on s'est r'perdu d'vue
(When we met I knew what she knew too
Then we lost touch, then we met anew)

Medium shot of ALBERT *and* CATHERINE.

On s'est retrouvé, on s'est réchauffé,

67

Puis on s'est séparé.
Chacun pour soi est reparti
Dans l'tourbillon de la vie.
(And warmed each other, just one night,
Then again lost sight.
We just went on a different way
Blown apart by life one day)
Je l'ai revue un soir, haïe, haïe, haïe
Ca fait déjà un fameux bail (twice)
Au son des bandjos je l'ai reconnue.
(Then I saw her again and oh, and oh
It seemed so long ago
Till we met again where the banjos play,)
Close-up of CATHERINE.
Ce curieux sourire qui m'avait tant plu.
Sa voix si fatale, son beau visage pâle
M'émurent plus que jamais.
Je me suis saoulé en l'écoutant.
L'alcool fait oublier le temps.
Je me suis réveillé en sentant
(That odd smile I'd loved before
That voice so light, that face so white
Enchanted me once more
She spoke and my heart began to race
I forgot the time, I forgot the place
As I woke up in her embrace)
Close-up of ALBERT *playing the guitar.*
Des baisers sur mon front brûlant (twice)
On s'est connu, on s'est reconnu.
(I felt her kisses on my face
When we met, I knew what she knew too.)
Close-up of CATHERINE.
On s'est perdu de vue, on s'est r'perdu de vue
On s'est retrouvé, on s'est séparé.
(But then we lost touch, then we met anew
Then we met again, and all was right)
Medium shot of ALBERT *and* CATHERINE.
Puis on s'est réchauffé.

Chacun pour soi est reparti,
Dans l'tourbillon de la vie.
Je l'ai revue un soir à là là
Elle est retombé dans mes bras.
(Then again lost sight
We just went on a different way
Blown apart by life one day
Until we met again one night, and well
Into my arms she fell)
Close-up of CATHERINE.
Quand on s'est connu
Quand on s'est reconnu
Pourquoi se perdre de vue
Se reperdre de vue
(When the first time you knew
And the second time too
It was just right for you
What's parting got to do?)

Quand on s'est retrouvé
Quand on s'est réchauffé
Pourquoi se séparer?
(When you feel in your heart
That it's right from the start,
Then you mustn't part.)

Alors tous deux on est reparti
Dans le tourbillon de la vie
(So we set off together anew
Spinning through life, just me and you)

On a continué à tourner
Tous les deux enlacés
Tous les deux enlacés.
(And we whirl through life this way
Embracing till this day,
Embracing till this day.)
At the end of the song, the camera pans across to JULES
and the shot dissolves to another of the four friends

69

riding along on bicycles, with SABINE *sitting on* JIM'S *crossbar. The camera tracks along backwards in front of them. They are riding very fast down a gentle slope,* ALBERT *and* CATHERINE *in front, then* JIM *with* SABINE, *and* JULES *last.* (*Still on page 62*)

VOICE *off* : As she meant something different to each of the three men, Catherine could not hope to please the three of them together, and she did not care. Jim felt out of place. He could only admire Catherine unreservedly by herself. In company, she became something relative.

ALBERT *leaves them at a cross-roads with a friendly wave of the hand. Close-up of* JIM *watching* CATHERINE *from behind. The camera pans briefly and comes to rest on* CATHERINE.

JIM *and* CATHERINE *are seen coming out of the chalet at night. The camera tracks sideways to follow them in medium close-up.*

CATHERINE : Our affection for each other has only just begun. We must leave it in peace like a new-born child. You have been in love, Jim, very much so. I can feel it. Why didn't you marry her?

JIM : It just didn't turn out like that.

CATHERINE : What is she like?

JIM : Sensible and patient. She says she will wait for me for ever. Her name is Gilberte.

CATHERINE : You still love her and she loves you. Don't make her suffer, Jim.

They stop underneath the balcony. JIM *moves close to* CATHERINE *and kisses her on the back of the neck.*

JIM : I feel the need for adventures, for risks. And then there is something new. I admire you Catherine, I enjoy coming to see you. *Close-up of* CATHERINE *and* JIM. I am afraid of forgetting about Jules.

CATHERINE : You mustn't forget him, you must warn him.

The camera pans upwards to reveal JULES *standing on the balcony.*

JULES *declaiming* : Alle das Neigen
                   Von Herzen zu Herzen

Ach wie so eigen
Schaffet das Schmerzen.
There is a moment's silence, then JULES *speaks again.*
JULES : Catherine . . . Translate!
Shot of CATHERINE *and* JIM *from the balcony, as seen by*
JULES.
CATHERINE : All these hearts reaching out towards each other,
Oh my God, my God, what pain they cause.
Alternate shots of JULES, CATHERINE *and* JIM, *following
the dialogue.*
JULES : Not bad . . . although you put in the ' my God, my
God ' . . . Good night, and if you meet the others, give them
my regards.
CATHERINE : Jules, I would like to read *Les Affinités* this
evening. Can you lend it to me?
JULES : I've just lent it to Jim.
CATHERINE : Too bad.
JULES closes the shutters and CATHERINE *and* JIM *take
their leave of each other. As* CATHERINE *is going into the
house,* JIM *calls after her.*
JIM : I'll bring it tomorrow.
Dissolve to an interior shot of the inn where JIM *is
staying. It is daytime. A telephone is ringing in the foreground. The proprietress comes and lifts the receiver.*
PROPRIETRESS : Hello. Just wait a moment, please. *Calling:*
Monsieur Jim, you're wanted on the telephone at once.
*JIM appears immediately and comes across to the tele-
phone. Close-up of* JULES *at the telephone in the chalet.*
JULES : Jim, you must bring back *Les Affinités.* Catherine
insists on reading it this evening. Jim, Catherine has had
enough of me. I'm terrified of losing her, that she'll go out
of my life altogether. The last time I saw you side by side
with Catherine, you were like a married couple. *A pause.* Jim,
love her, marry her, and let me see her. I mean to say, if you
love her, stop thinking of me as an obstacle.
Return to JIM *at the inn. Close-up of his hand picking
up a book with the title ' Les Affinités Electives.'*
Cut to an exterior shot of the chalet at night. JIM *ap-*

proaches and goes up the steps towards the door, where CATHERINE *is waiting for him. She leads him inside. The camera follows them from behind. In close-up, they turn towards each other and we see them in profile against a window.* JIM *caresses* CATHERINE'S *face, runs his finger down her profile (Still on page 63), reaches her mouth and kisses it. (Still on page 64)*

In the next shot, they are seen lying down on a divan. (Still on page 64) They are inside the chalet. It is night.

VOICE *off* : All day long, Jim had hoped for this moment. Catherine was in his arms, on his knees, talking in her low voice. Their first kiss lasted the rest of the night.

Slow dissolve to two close-ups of CATHERINE.

VOICE *off* : They did not talk, they reached out towards one another. Towards dawn, they reached their goal. Catherine's expression was full of curiosity and an extraordinary jubilation.

The camera pans across the book ' Les Affinités Electives,' then upwards to the window. Outside, dawn is breaking.

VOICE *off* : When Jim got up, he was enslaved. Other women no longer existed for him.

Fade out.

Shot of the terrace outside the chalet. It is daytime. JULES *and* SABINE *are sitting at the table playing dominoes, with breakfast cups beside them. (Still on page 81)*

CATHERINE *off* : Jules.

The camera pans vertically up to show CATHERINE *at the window.* JULES *gets up and goes towards the door where she appears again. She kisses him in medium close-up, then turns towards* JIM *as he also comes out of the door.*

CATHERINE : I have asked Jim to come and live here altogether. He will have the small bedroom.

CATHERINE moves out of frame; JULES *and* JIM *go towards the table.*

JULES : Take care, Jim. Take care for her and for yourself.

They sit down, and the scene dissolves to a shot of JIM *coming out of the inn, followed by* CATHERINE *and by*

JULES *carrying* JIM's *luggage. The camera pans away from the inn towards the chalet.*
Inside the chalet they are seen mounting the staircase with MATHILDE.

CATHERINE *to* MATHILDE : Mathilde, Sie können uns lassen, ich mache das selbst fertig. (*Subtitle* : *You can leave us, Mathilde, I'll finish that off myself.*)

MATHILDE *goes down the staircase again.* JULES *goes into his study-bedroom with* SABINE, *while* CATHERINE *opens the door of the room* JIM *is to occupy and goes in followed by* JIM.

CATHERINE *inside the room*: Here is your improvised bedroom. Those books are German . . . but you'll find others in my room; the wardrobe . . . I'll unpack the cases.

With this brief inventory of the room, she notices that he has put his hat down on the bed. She removes it immediately . . . then looks around as if wondering whether she has forgotten anything.

CATHERINE : I think that will do more or less. That bit over there is a mess anyway . . . but it can't be helped.

JIM : What is there behind it?

CATHERINE : Sabine and Mathilde's bedroom. *A pause.* The bed isn't too bad. Come and sit down beside me.

They go and sit down on the bed in medium close-up.

JIM : I've always loved the back of your neck.

CATHERINE *lifts up her hair and* JIM *kisses her on the back of her neck.*

JIM : The only part of you I could look at without being seen.

In an outhouse near the chalet, JULES *is seen from above, sawing up logs.**

SABINE *is standing beside him holding out her arms while* JULES *loads her up with the sawn wood. She goes out of the door and up the steps to the house. Pan as she walks along the terrace; then, with the camera still panning, cut to* JIM *and* CATHERINE *walking in the forest.*

---

* Truffaut cut this scene in some copies of the film distributed both in France and abroad.

JIM: And Jules?

CATHERINE: He loves both of us. He won't be surprised and this way he will suffer less. We will love and respect him.

Dissolve to the terrace outside the chalet. Medium close-up of CATHERINE *pointing at* JIM. *The camera tracks in a circle round the table, at which are seated* JULES, JIM *and* SABINE, *stopping on each of them briefly in close-up before moving on.* SABINE *is making faces. Hold on close-ups of* JIM *and* CATHERINE, *watching her and laughing.*

VOICE *off*: In the village, down at the bottom of the valley, the trio were known as 'the three lunatics,' but apart from that, they were well liked. When Catherine learnt of this, she invented a game which they called 'the village idiot.' The village was the table, and they took it in turns to be the idiot. Sabine, in particular, reduced them to hysterical laughter.

In the next shot, we are inside the chalet. It is evening. CATHERINE, *at the bottom of the stairs, kisses* JULES *and then goes up. The camera follows her; close-up of the back of her head. She joins* JIM *on the landing and kisses him.*

VOICE *off*: Catherine had said: 'One is never completely in love for more than a moment,' but for her that moment came again and again.

It is daytime. Shot of SABINE *dozing in a hammock on the terrace, then pan to* CATHERINE *opening her window.*

VOICE *off*: Life was one long holiday. Never had Jules and Jim spent so much time playing dominoes. Time passed . . . A period of happiness holds little that can be related . . . it gradually uses itself up without anyone noticing the usury.

Shot from the terrace outside the chalet, through the window into the living room. JIM *is reading, rocking to and fro in the rocking-chair. He raises his head, as laughter and joyful cries are heard from* JULES *and* CATHERINE, *off.*

VOICE *off*: One Sunday, Catherine decided to seduce Jules. While Jim was reading a book downstairs, she led Jules up

to her room. ' No, no, no ! ' Jules kept saying. ' Yes, yes, yes ! '
Catherine insisted.

*In the next shot, with the camera on a crane at first-
floor level, we see* CATHERINE'S *window from the outside.
We move forward into the room.* JULES *and* CATHERINE
are struggling on the bed. Catherine is on top of JULES
. . . and despite JULES'S *protests, they are both laughing
happily. (Still on page 81)*

Return to JIM, *pacing nervously to and fro in the living
room.*

VOICE *off* : In vain did Jim tell himself that he had no right
to be jealous; he realised that he was all the same. Catherine
noticed this and did not repeat the experiment . . . or the day
off.

The next sequence opens with a shot of JULES, *with*
SABINE *sitting astride his shoulders, and* JIM *and* CATHER-
INE, *as they cross a bridge at the edge of a lake.*

*They are seen again in long shot on the bank, picking up
pebbles and bouncing them across the surface of the
water.*

VOICE *off* : Together the four of them walked round the lake,
a stretch of water shrouded in mist at the bottom of a humid
and lush valley. The harmony between them was complete.
Catherine had a migraine, which passed. Jim, who was worn
out, had a succession of them which were worse. He thought :
if we had children, they would be tall and thin and would
suffer from migraines. They went down to the water's edge
and started playing with the white pebbles on the shore.
Catherine made Jim throw them until he was exhausted. She
and Jules learned how to bounce them across the water. The
sky seemed close above their heads.

Cut to a high shot of the little country station. JIM *is
seen putting his luggage on to the train, which is about
to leave. Then he embraces* JULES *and* CATHERINE. *The
train starts to move . . .* CATHERINE *runs alongside it
for a moment, the camera following from above in a
helicopter.*

VOICE *off* : Jim was needed back in Paris. His newspaper was demanding his return. The departure would have been agonising for them without the certainty that they would come together again soon, intact, exactly as they had left each other. The month they had spent together was graven in their memories by a multitude of small but perfect details. When the train moved off, they waved gently to each other for a long time. Jules had given them a kind of blessing, and had embraced Jim, who had entrusted Catherine to him in parting . . . for they wanted to marry and have children.

Back in Paris, JIM *is seen sitting at a café table with Gilberte.*

JIM : Jules agrees to a quick divorce. I am going to marry Catherine. I want to have children by her. Jules will find work for me in his country. I am in the middle of translating a play which is on in Vienna and which is going to be put on here. GILBERTE *picks up her bag and makes as if to get up.*

JIM : Where are you going?

GILBERTE : I'm going home.

JIM : I'll come with you.

GILBERTE : No, really . . . I'd rather you didn't.

She gets up and goes quickly out of the café. Looking upset, JIM *goes after her, but as he moves across the café, he is stopped by an elegantly-dressed young woman. The camera frames the two of them in medium close-up.*

THERESE : Hello, Jim . . . It's Thérèse . . . the steam-engine. *She puts her cigarette in her mouth the wrong way round.*

JIM : Hello, Thérèse. How are you? . . . How is . . .

THERESE : It was fine for two weeks. But I deceived him so I could buy him a great big Meerschaum pipe carved with the head of Vercingétorix . . . his dream! He found out. Jealous, didn't trust me. Locked me up for three weeks, they called me the Prisoner of Cholet. I was flattered at first, then got fed up. So I hopped it through the window with a ladder belonging to a house-painter — who I seduced. We set up house together, but I got the fidgets.

As THERESE *pours out her story, someone comes up to* JIM.

THE MAN: Hello, Jim. How are things? And your pal?

JIM: Fine.

THERESE continues her story, oblivious of the interruption.

THERESE: A fellow promised me a fortune. I followed him, went off with him, got as far as Cairo where I found myself in an establishment . . . yes, an establishment where I acted the virgin. The place was raided by the police, and seeing my age, they put me in the care of some nuns. I met an Englishman who wanted to save me. I lived with him in a villa on the Red Sea, with a tennis court and horses. There I got a letter from my village: my cousin was going to marry a girl from the neighbouring town.

There is another interruption, which again does not stem the flow from THERESE.

JIM *recognising the man who has come up to him*: Hello.

THE FRIEND: Is Jules in Paris?

JIM: No, he didn't come.

THERESE *continuing*: I remembered the cousin. I liked him. So suddenly, wham! Delayed action, I'm head over heels in love. I dropped everything and went back to the village to break up the marriage. I married him. After three months, I was fed up . . . So I came back to Paris. I met an undertaker, nice man. I chased him but he didn't want to know. My husband divorced me for desertion. So finally the undertaker married me, convinced at last. We make a perfect couple, but we've no children. He's the only man I can't deceive . . . because he doesn't leave me the time or the energy.

A third friend of JIM's passes.

THE FRIEND: Hello, Jim. How's your pal? Still with the same girl? . . . Wouldn't mind having a go at her myself, no sir!

THERESE: Finally I'm writing my memoirs for the European edition of the *Sunday Time Magazine* . . . And there we are!

Pan towards the door of the café: a small man with a moustache enters, wearing a black hat.

THERESE: This is my husband . . . And you, Jim?

JIM: Me, I'm going to get married. *She flings herself at him.*

THERESE: No!

JIM : Yes.

JIM extricates himself from her and turns to the husband.

JIM : Au revoir, *Monsieur.*

THE HUSBAND : Cheers.

Leaving the front room of the café, JIM *is stopped by yet another acquaintance. The camera tracks forwards to frame the two of them. A girl can be seen at the edge of the screen on the left.*

THE ACQUAINTANCE : Hello, Jim. How is Jules?

JIM : Fine.

THE ACQUAINTANCE : Interesting, isn't she? She's called Denise. It's no use talking to her, she won't answer. In fact, she never speaks. She's not a half-wit, she's just empty. *The man flicks at the girl's head; she doesn't move.* There's nothing in there. She's just a thing.

JIM : A beautiful thing!

THE ACQUAINTANCE : Yes, a beautiful object. *Close-up of the girl, as the voice continues off.* She's sex personified, pure sex . . . Come on, Denise, say au revoir to the gentleman.

THE GIRL : *Monsieur.*

JIM : Au revoir, *Mademoiselle.*

Fade out.

Shot of the living room of the chalet from the outside. It is night. Through the window we see CATHERINE *reading a letter by the fireside.*

VOICE *off* : Catherine spent the winter at the chalet sitting in front of log fires. She was Jim's fiancée, left in the care of Jules. Every day she asked Jules : ' Do you think Jim loves me? '

Shot of GILBERTE'S *apartment at night.* JIM *and* GILBERTE *are lying in bed awake.*

JIM : Listen, Gilberte, you see . . . once Catherine wants to do something, so long as she thinks that it won't hurt anyone else — she can be mistaken, of course — she does it for her own enjoyment, and to learn something from it. That way she hopes to become wise.

GILBERTE : That could go on for a long time.

JIM : Don't be mean, Gilberte. *He turns the light out.*

GILBERTE: I'm not being mean. I'm jealous. I've always known this is what would happen . . . *A pause* . . . Jim, don't go tomorrow. She will have you for the rest of her life. Give me one more week. *They kiss.*

VOICE *off*: Jim could no more leave Gilberte than Catherine could Jules. Jules must not suffer, nor must Gilberte. They were two different fruits from the past, which complemented and counterbalanced each other.

> *Return to the living room of the chalet. It is evening.* CATHERINE, *wearing her spectacles, is reading a letter from* JIM *out to* JULES, *who is rocking to and fro in his chair.*

CATHERINE *reading*: 'Tell Jules I have seen Thérèse again. She is married now and a woman of letters. I must put off my return again, but I shall soon be free. I still have one or two more farewells to make.' *A pause* . . . One or two farewells! . . . Do you think Jim loves me?

> JIM *is seen getting out of the train at the country station at night.* JULES, *a little embarrassed, is waiting for him near the exit. The two friends embrace, then walk together towards the camera.*

JIM: What's happened? Why hasn't Catherine come to meet me?

JULES: She wasn't too pleased with your letters. You talked too much about your work, about your farewells. Catherine doesn't like people being away from her. You have been away too long. When she has the slightest doubt, she always goes much further than the other person.

> *The camera pans and then tracks to follow them.*

JIM: But she's waiting for us at the chalet?

JULES: Yes, I think so . . . Of course.

> *In the next shot, the two men are seen entering the living room of the chalet. It is empty.* JULES *looks into the kitchen.*

JULES: Catherine!

> *Looking upset, he goes up the stairs. The camera holds on* JIM *in close-up, who looks up as* JULES *comes down the stairs again, looking sad and confused.*

79

JULES : I didn't want to tell you. She left yesterday morning without any explanation. I was hoping she would have come back before you arrived.

The two men go back into the living room. JIM *takes off his coat, while* JULES *fetches a letter from the writing table. They sit down.*

JIM : You're not worried?

JULES : You mean, in case something has happened to her? . . . No, I just think that she is in the process of doing something irreparable. I have already told you that your letter didn't go down very well. ' I have seen Thérèse again. She is married now and a woman of letters . . . I still have one or two farewells to make . . .' *Medium close-up of* JULES. . . . No, no, Jim, . . . you know very well; all the things Catherine does, she does fully, one by one. She is a force of nature, she expresses herself in cataclysms. Wherever she is, she lives surrounded by her own brightness and harmony, guided by the conviction of her own innocence.

JIM *in close-up* : You talk of her as if she were a queen!

Alternate close-ups of JULES *and* JIM, *following the dialogue.*

JULES : But she *is* a queen Jim! I tell you frankly. Catherine is neither particularly beautiful, nor intelligent, nor sincere, but she is a real woman . . . and she is a woman we love . . . and whom all men desire. Why, after all, should a woman as sought-after as Catherine have chosen to grace us with her presence? Because we give her our undivided attention, as we would to a queen.

JIM : I will admit to you Jules . . . I almost didn't come back from Paris. I knew things would never be the same between us; even our friendship is strained by it. At times, I feel jealous of you, of your years of happiness with her, and sometimes I detest you for not being jealous of me.

JULES : Do you really believe that, Jim? I will stop at nothing to avoid losing Catherine altogether, and you will be like me when she comes back . . . for she always comes back.

JIM *gets up and the camera tracks backwards to bring the two men into frame.* JIM *puts on his hat and coat again.*

JIM: Tell her that you went to meet me at the station, but I wasn't there. I have decided . . . it's the only solution.

JULES: Yes . . . that's it: I went to the station, but you weren't there.

A slight noise is heard off, from the window. Close-up of CATHERINE *looking in at the two men and tapping on the window pane. (Still on page 82) She is smiling. Medium close-up of* JULES *and* JIM, *both wearing a slightly strangled expression. The camera pans across to the door as* CATHERINE *comes in.*

CATHERINE: Hello . . . Well, what's the matter with you? *To* JIM. Have you just arrived?

She kisses JULES, *then* JIM, *and calmly takes off her coat. Fade out.*

The next image fades in to show CATHERINE *and* JIM *in bed in* CATHERINE'S *room. It is night.*

CATHERINE: There, now you are my Jim and I am your Catherine. Everything is all right. It was just that in your letters you talked too much about your own affairs; I have mine too. You talked about saying good-bye to your old loves, so I went to say good-bye to mine. You'll hold me in your arms all night, but no more. We want to have a child, don't we, Jim? Well, if you gave me one now, I wouldn't know if it was yours. You understand, Jim?

JIM *turns towards the wall. (Still on page 83)*

CATHERINE: I had to do it.

JIM: Do you love Albert?

CATHERINE: No.

JIM: And does he love you?

CATHERINE: Yes, Jim. Believe me, it's the only way we can start off on the right footing. Albert equals Gilberte. *A moment's silence.* You've nothing to say? We must start again from scratch.

VOICE *off*: Pay off your debts and start again from scratch: that was the basis of Catherine's philosophy. They lay there, trembling and chaste. Catherine went to sleep, while Jim remained with his eyes open in the dark. He realised that she loved him just as he loved her, that they were both drawn to each other by the same force. Once more they started again from scratch, again they soared upwards like great birds of prey. *Dissolve to an aerial tracking shot of the chalet, taken from a helicopter.* They had to remain chaste, until Catherine was certain that she was not bearing Albert's child. This self-imposed restraint left them in a state of exaltation. They remained constantly together. They did not cheat. The promised land was in sight. *The camera tracks backwards, away from the chalet.* The promised land suddenly retreated. When the moment for conceiving the child came at last, Catherine did not become pregnant. *Rapid shot from above of* CATHERINE *and* JIM *coming out of a doctor's surgery into the street.* They went to see a specialist who told them that they must be patient, and that many couples did not conceive for months.

Fade out.

It is night. CATHERINE *is lying in bed in her room.* JIM *gets into bed and kisses her. She turns away.*

JIM : What's the matter?

CATHERINE : I want to sleep alone tonight. Go to your room.

JIM : But why?

CATHERINE : That's how it is.

JIM : Explain yourself.

CATHERINE : There's nothing to explain.

JIM : I'll lie beside you, like this. I won't touch you.

CATHERINE : That's not true . . . and anyway, I don't care. I'm disgusted. Every evening's a nightmare. I keep thinking about this child which we will never have . . . I feel as if I'm trying to pass an exam; I can't stand it any longer.

JIM : But we love each other, Catherine, and that's all that matters.

CATHERINE : No. I count too, and I don't love so much. So let us make an honest attempt to do without each other. If we part and I find out afterwards that I still love you, that's my affair. Go on, go back to Gilberte, since she writes to you every day. *She gets out of bed and puts on her dressing-gown.*

JIM : You're not being fair, Catherine.

CATHERINE : No doubt, but I am a heartless person. That

86

is why I don't love you and shall never love anyone. And then I'm thirty-two and you are twenty-nine. When you are forty, you will want a woman. I shall be forty-three. You'll find one of twenty-five . . . and I shall be left alone like an idiot.

She goes towards the door.

JIM : Perhaps you are right, Catherine . . . I'll leave tomorrow. Let us separate for three months.

CATHERINE : Are you sad? Then I shall stop being sad, because we mustn't both suffer at the same time. When you stop, I shall start again.

She goes quickly out of the room and knocks on JULES'S *door.*

CATHERINE *going in* : Jules? Am I disturbing you?

Cut to the inside of JULES'S *room. He turns towards her, but he does not reply.*

CATHERINE : I've had enough. Did you hear us arguing?

She sits on JULES'S *bed, which is still made.*

JULES : No, I was working. *He sits down beside her.*

CATHERINE : I can't stand him any longer. I'm going mad. Anyway, he's leaving tomorrow. Good riddance!

JULES : Don't be unjust, Catherine . . . You know that he loves you.

CATHERINE : I don't know any longer, I really don't. He lied to me. He didn't dare break it off with Gilberte. He doesn't know himself what he thinks : ' You love her, you don't love her, you'll love her in the end.' After all, it's not my fault if we don't have a child.

JULES : Have you got a cigarette?

She gives him a cigarette and lights it for him.

JULES : Do you want me to go and speak to him?

CATHERINE : No, that's the last thing I want. I'm half with him, half against him, but I want him to go. We have decided to separate for three months. What do you think?

JULES : I don't know. Perhaps it's a good idea.

CATHERINE : You don't want to tell me what you think. I know you really despise me.

JULES : No, Catherine, I never despise you.

He moves closer to her and caresses her face.

87

JULES : I shall always love you, whatever you do, whatever happens.

>CATHERINE *flings herself against him. Close-up of the two of them. (Still on page 83)*

CATHERINE : Oh Jules, is that true? I love you, too. *She kisses him.* We have been really happy together, the two of us, haven't we?

JULES : But we are still happy . . . at least, I am.

>*She starts to weep and he kisses her.*

CATHERINE : Yes. We'll stay together always, like two little old people, with Sabine and Sabine's little children. Keep me close to you. I don't want to go back to him before he leaves.

JULES : Stay here then . . . I will go and sleep downstairs.

>*He gets up, in close-up, and goes towards the door. The camera tracks forward with him, and tracks backwards as he comes back again abruptly. He takes* CATHERINE *in his arms and kisses her.*

JULES : My poor little Catherine! You often remind me of a Chinese play I saw before the war. When the curtain rises, the emperor leans confidentially towards the audience and says : 'You see in me the most unhappy of men, for I have two wives : the first wife and the second wife.'

>*They weep gently in each other's arms. (Still on page 84) Then* CATHERINE *lies down on the bed.* JULES *gets up and goes out of the room.*
>
>*Cut to the living room, where* JULES *has settled himself in his rocking chair in front of the log fire.*

VOICE *off* : Thus for Jules, their love was becoming something relative, while his own remained absolute.

>*Cut to an exterior shot of the chalet at dawn. A thick mist hangs over the house and the surrounding forest. At the bottom of the steps,* JIM *says goodbye to* JULES *and* SABINE *. . . Then* JIM *and* CATHERINE *go off together. (Still on page 84)*

VOICE *off* : The next morning Jim left the house. Catherine wanted once more to accompany him to the station. In the night, the mist had descended upon the meadow. The rest of the hive, not knowing of the situation, realised vaguely that Jim was out of favour with their queen. Thus his departure was to be expected.

After they have gone a short distance, CATHERINE *turns round.*

CATHERINE : The house is already out of sight.

Fade out.

CATHERINE *and* JIM *are seen entering a hotel room. It is daytime.*

VOICE *off* : The timetable had just been changed for the autumn; there was no train until the following day.

CATHERINE : One always feels guilty in hotel rooms. I may not be very moral, but I don't have a taste for secrecy. You do. Don't deny it, I won't believe you.

JIM does not reply, but draws the curtains, then goes towards the bed. CATHERINE, *seen in medium close-up, takes off her make-up in front of a mirror, in which we can see the reflection of* JIM *lying on the bed and watching her.*

VOICE *off* : Jim thought of the children he might have had by Catherine. He imagined each of them more handsome than the last, a big house full of them. He also told himself : ' If we don't have any children, Catherine will start her adventures again.'

Close-up of CATHERINE *in the mirror, taking off her make-up.*

VOICE *off* : They did not speak to each other . . . and it was in this cold and dreary hotel room that they took each other once more, without knowing why, perhaps as a kind of full stop. It was like a burial, or as if they were already dead. For the first time, Jim was presented with the spectacle of Catherine lying frigid and motionless, and he gave himself to her reluctantly. The next day Catherine accompanied Jim to the train, but they did not wave their handkerchiefs in farewell. They parted from each other in anguish, yet nothing was forcing them to do so.

Aerial shot of the train moving away from the station and gathering speed.

VOICE *off* : Once more, Jim thought that it was all finished.

Exterior shots of Paris in the daytime: from a lift in the Eiffel Tower, then from the Métro as it crosses the Seine and passes a window.

Interior shot of GILBERTE'S *bedroom.* JIM *is in bed.* GILBERTE *comes into view bearing a tray, a steaming jug and a towel. The camera pans across to the bed.*

GILBERTE : Here's your inhaler. There's a letter too.

JIM *tears open the letter and his voice is heard off.*

JIM *reading to himself* : ' I think I am pregnant. Come quickly. Catherine.' *A pause, then he calls out.* Gilberte, will you bring me some writing paper, please.

Dissolve to close-up of JIM's *hand, writing.*

JIM *off* : Catherine, I am in bed ill and in no state to get up. Nor have I any desire to come and see you, probably pregnant by someone else . . . for our last pitiful farewell cannot have succeeded where our love at its best failed.

Cut to the living room of the chalet. It is evening. CATHERINE *is seated in the rocking-chair.* JULES *is reading the end of* JIM's *letter.*

JULES : ' . . . at its best failed.'

He looks up at his wife, then goes over to the table, sits down and takes a sheet of writing paper.

JULES : You are right. I don't believe a word of this talk about illness. I shall write to him straight away and say that you want to see him. *He writes.* ' Dear hypochondriac, come and see us as soon as possible. Catherine is expecting a letter from you. Write very large as her eyes are strained . . .'

Cut to JIM's *room in Paris.*

JULES *off* : ' . . . and she can only read large writing . . .'

JIM : ' Catherine thinks that I wasn't really ill. I myself wonder if she is really pregnant. In any case, it is unlikely that I am the father. I have every justification for my doubts, our past, Albert . . . and all the rest.'

Jim folds the letter, seals the envelope and hands it to GILBERTE *as she appears beside the bed.*

JIM : Would you post this letter for me, as you're going out?

GILBERTE : Of course.

She departs . . . The camera pans to follow her as far

90

as the front door, where several letters are lying on the mat. The camera pans back again with her, as she picks them up and carries them back to the bed.

GILBERTE : Look, there's a letter for you. *She gives it to him and goes off again.* I must go, I shall be late. See you later.

She shuts the door behind her, while JIM *examines the letter and opens it.*

Aerial view of wooded countryside with an image of CATHERINE'S *face superimposed on it. She recites the letter as* JIM *reads.*

CATHERINE : ' I love you, Jim. There are so many things on this earth which we do not understand . . . and so many unbelievable things which are true . . . At last I am fertile . . . Let us thank God, Jim, bow down before Him. I am sure, absolutely sure that you are the father. I beseech you to believe me. Your love is a part of my life. You are living inside me. Believe me, Jim, believe me. This paper is your skin, this ink is my blood. I am pressing hard so that it may enter in. Answer me quickly.'

JIM *leaps out of bed, goes to the window and opens it.*

JIM *calling* : Gilberte !

Medium close-up of JIM *sitting at a table on the terrace of a café, writing.*

JIM *writing* : ' My love, I believe you. I believe in you. I am preparing to leave for you. When I find a small piece of goodness inside me, I know that it comes from you.'

VOICE *off* : Once, they had promised never to telephone each other, for fear of hearing each other's voices without being able to touch. Their letters took three days in the post. It was like a conversation between two deaf people.

Shot of CATHERINE, *in her room in the chalet, finishing* JIM's *letter.*

CATHERINE *reading* : ' I have every justification for my doubts, our past, Albert . . . and all the rest.'

She immediately picks up her pen to reply.

CATHERINE *writing* : ' I will stop thinking about you so that you will stop thinking about me. You disgust me now, which is wrong, for one should never be disgusted by anything.'

91

A street in Paris: rapid shot of JIM *putting a letter in a letter box.*

Rapid exterior shot of the chalet, at night, then cut to CATHERINE, *at her table in medium close-up, as she writes a letter.*

CATHERINE *writing*: 'My darling Jim, your long letter has changed everything. This morning I said to myself: in two days, instead of a miserable letter, he will be here himself. Let us forget quickly the harsh words of the day before yesterday. Now there is no place for them. Jim, come when you can . . . but make it soon. Come even in the middle of the night.'

Return to JIM *in his room in Paris, reading a letter.*

VOICE *off*: Finally Jim received a letter from Jules.

Rapid shot of JULES *in the living room of the chalet, reading aloud the letter he has just written, then resume on* JIM *in medium close-up.*

JULES: 'Your child has died after a third of his pre-natal existence. Catherine wants no further communication from you . . .'

VOICE *off*: Thus between the two of them, they had created nothing. Jim thought: 'It is a noble thing to want to rediscover the laws of humanity; but how convenient it must be to conform to existing rules. We played with the very sources of life, and we failed.'

Fade out.

Fade in to a series of exterior shots of Paris from the elevated Métro.

Long shot of the steps leading up to the gymnasium. JULES *passes* JIM *without seeing him. Suddenly he turns round and comes back towards* JIM, *throwing his arms in the air.*

JULES: It's unbelievable!

JIM: You've finally left the chalet?

JULES: Yes, we prefer to live in France now. We are renting an old mill on the banks of the Seine.

JIM: Jules, I insist that we meet again. Come to my place tomorrow. It would give me great pleasure.

JULES : Fine.

The camera pans across a poster advertising a boxing match.

*The scene dissolves to the interior of JIM's apartment. Close-up of the hands of JULES and JIM playing dominoes. The camera tracks backwards to reveal the two men in medium close-up. (Still on page 101)

JIM : Please tell me about Catherine.

Close-up of hands and dominoes. JULES is heard off.

JULES *off* : For a long time, I was afraid she would commit suicide. She had bought a revolver. She would say : ' So-and-so died of suicide,' just as one says : ' So-and-so died of cholera.' *The camera tracks backwards to a medium shot of the two men.* She withdrew into herself like a widow. It was as if she were recovering from a serious illness. She moved around very slowly with the fixed smile of a corpse.

Pan to GILBERTE, coming into the room. The two men get up.

JIM : Gilberte, may I introduce my friend Jules.

GILBERTE : Jim has talked about you so much that I feel I know you very well.

She leaves the room, while the camera holds on JULES and JIM.

JIM : Does Catherine know you have come to see me ?

JULES : Yes . . . She invites you out for a drive. I would like you to accept, and perhaps Madame as well ?

JIM : No, she wouldn't come. But I will.

JULES puts on his hat and goes to the door.

JULES : I must go now.

JIM *smiling* : Oh no, Jules, you can't wear a hat like that . . . at least not in France.

He takes JULES's hat off and replaces it with his own, which suits JULES much better.

JIM : Here, take mine.

JULES and JIM are seen again meeting outside a water-

---

* In May 1962, François Truffaut cut the following scene in several copies distributed in France and abroad.

mill. The camera pans away from them to frame the mill, standing surrounded by greenery in the middle of the countryside.

JULES : This way up.

They climb a flight of steps to the door of the mill.

JULES : She is in a very good mood this morning . . . Above all, don't upset her.

JIM looks out across the river bank and the surrounding countryside. The camera pans, following his gaze.

JIM *off* : It's marvellous here.

The camera pans further and comes to rest on a motor car.

JULES *off* : That's Catherine's car.

Return to JULES and JIM going into the mill. Inside CATHERINE is folding some linen. JULES presents JIM to her as if he were introducing them for the first time.

JULES : It's Jim.

CATHERINE *shaking his hand* : Hello.

CATHERINE greets JIM as if they had only parted the previous day. Then, with the two men standing beside her, she carefully folds up her nightdress, making a little parcel. JULES and JIM exchange glances behind her back.

VOICE *off* : Catherine was gay and smiling, but she wore the secret look which announced one of her evenings of intrigue. She took her white nightdress and tied it up neatly with a small ribbon . . . Jim wondered what the purpose of the nightdress was, then forgot about it. They set off for a walk.

Pan as CATHERINE goes out followed by JULES and JIM. Outside, we see them come down the staircase and go towards the car. Close-up of CATHERINE'S hand on the starter, then of her foot on the accelerator. The car moves off, and the camera pans after it. (Still on page 101) Dissolve to a long shot of the Seine valley. Following the road, the car winds across the countryside. Medium close-up of the road, then of the bonnet of the car. It stops in front of an inn.

CATHERINE *who now wears her glasses all the time* : Oh, I'm so hungry. Shall we have dinner here?

Close-up of CATHERINE *putting on the handbrake. They get out (Still on page 102) and walk towards the inn,* JIM *still carrying* CATHERINE'S *parcel. On the way* CATHERINE *stops for a moment to remove a stone from her shoe. The camera tracks sideways, preceding them to the door of the inn where* ALBERT *is standing.*

CATHERINE : Good Lord, Albert! What are you doing here?

ALBERT : I'm getting some fresh air. Anyway, I live here.

He points and the camera pans upwards to a first-floor window. (Still on page 102)

CATHERINE : Will you dine with us?

ALBERT : Certainly, if you're going to eat straight away.

CATHERINE : You have a date in town perhaps?

ALBERT : Perhaps!

Shot of the doorway. They enter and sit down at a table. Dissolve to another shot of them coming out after the meal. JULES, JIM *and* CATHERINE *walk towards the gate of the inn garden.* JIM *is still carrying the parcel.* CATHERINE *goes up to him and touches his arm.*

CATHERINE : Give me my parcel.

She takes it from him and goes back to ALBERT, *who takes her by the arm. They both go into the inn, and as they do so,* CATHERINE *turns briefly towards* JULES *and* JIM.

CATHERINE : Good night!

JULES *and* JIM, *completely taken aback, walk towards the car.*

JIM : Well-played once again: good curtain-line and business with the white nightdress. I hadn't expected it. I'm surprised she didn't choose a new man to play the part. Albert has done it so many times before.

JULES : Why? Albert was perfect for this evening.

They stop by the car and JIM *starts to get in.*

JULES : Leave her the car. Catherine's motto is : ' In a couple, one person at least must be faithful — the other one.'

JIM *moving away from the car*: You have seen that I don't live alone any more. I am going to marry Gilberte.

The two men are seen again walking along the road.

The camera pans and tracks after them.

JULES : You are more sensible than I am. You have realised that with Catherine, once an affair is over, it is over for good. *A pause.* I think Gilberte will make a very good wife. She's very attractive.

> *Cut to* JIM'S *apartment.* JIM *is lying in bed asleep, next to* GILBERTE. *The sound of a motor horn wakes him. He hurries to the window with the camera panning after him. At first he can see nothing. Then he sees* CATHER- INE'S *car. Shot from* JIM'S *window, of the car moving across the open space in the middle of the deserted square, zig-zagging round benches, lamp-posts and trees.*

VOICE *off* : Jim recognised the rhythmic sound of the horn of Catherine's car in the distance. At first he could see nothing, then he noticed the car moving between the trees, wandering round the deserted square, brushing the benches and trees, like a horse without a rider or a phantom ship.

> *After a final blast on the horn, the car is driven back onto the road and disappears.* JIM *comes away from the window. Dissolve to close-up of* JIM *sleeping beside* GILBERTE. *The telephone rings.* JIM *wakes up and lifts the receiver.*
>
> *Long shot of the watermill, then a shot of* CATHERINE'S *bedroom. She is lying on the bed, talking into the telephone.*

CATHERINE : What a night I had. I don't know what I was doing there. That kind of life was dead for me. It was a desert, Jim, somewhere to die in. I talked about you, I searched for you . . . *A pause* . . . Are you listening? . . . It is you, isn't it? . . .

> *Rapid close-up of* JIM *hanging up the receiver and getting out of bed. Return to* CATHERINE *still holding the tele- phone.*

CATHERINE : Then come straightaway.

> *Dissolve to shot of* CATHERINE'S *car standing outside the mill. Pan as* JIM *climbs the staircase to the door.* CATHER- INE *draws him inside.*
>
> *Interior shot of* CATHERINE'S *room in the mill.* CATHER-

96

INE *and* JIM *sit down on the bed.* CATHERINE *tries to embrace him, but he gets up.*

CATHERINE : Come and lie beside me, kiss me.

JIM : Catherine, I have something to say to you, it's rather long.

CATHERINE : Tell me.

Low-angled shot of JIM.

JIM : In a novel you lent me I found a passage which you had marked. It was about a woman on a ship who gives herself in her imagination to a passenger she does not know. That struck me as a confession on your part. It's your method of exploring the universe. I have this lightning curiosity too; perhaps everyone has. But I control mine for your sake, and I am not convinced that you control yours for mine. Like you, I think that, in love, the couple is not ideal. One has only to look around one. JIM *goes towards the back of the room.* You wanted to construct something better, refusing hypocrisy and resignation. You wanted to invent love from the beginning . . . but pioneers should be humble, without egoism. *Rapid close-up of* JIM, *who is now near the window; then pan as he moves towards* CATHERINE *again.* No, we must look things straight in the face, Catherine. We have failed, we have made a mess of everything. You wanted to change me, to mould me to your needs. On my side, I have brought nothing but suffering to those around me, where I wanted to bring them joy. *He reaches the bed and sits down.* The promise I made to Gilberte that we would grow old together is worthless, because I can put it off indefinitely. It's a forgery. I no longer hope to marry you. I have to tell you, Catherine, I'm going to marry Gilberte. She and I can still have children.

Pan to CATHERINE, *smiling, in close-up.*

CATHERINE : A fine story, Jim! And me, Jim, what about me? And the children I wanted to have. You didn't want them, Jim!

Cut back to JIM, *then to reverse shot of* CATHERINE.

JIM : But I did, Catherine . . . I did.

CATHERINE : They would have been beautiful children, Jim! . . .

97

She sinks down on the bed, weeping, while JIM *watches her coldly. Then, suddenly, she gets up, producing a revolver from under the pillow.* JIM *also leaps to his feet, while* CATHERINE *runs across and locks the door. Close-up of her hand thowing the key out of the window. She turns round again and threatens* JIM *with the revolver.*

CATHERINE: You're going to die. You disgust me . . . I'm going to kill you, Jim. *A pause.* You're a coward, you're afraid . . .

> JIM *leaps at* CATHERINE, *seizes her arm and wrests the weapon from her, then jumps out of the window.*
> *Outside the mill, we see* JIM *landing on the ground. He runs off and the camera follows him for a moment from above . . . (Still on page 103)*
> *On the next image, the words 'Some months later' appear against a stormy sky, then dissolve to the façade of the Cinéma des Ursulines in Paris.*
> *Inside the cinema we see* JIM, *slightly from above, watching the screen. Quick shot of the screen: a newsreel shows a burning of books. The camera cuts back to* JIM, *then pans across the auditorium to reveal* JULES *and* CATHERINE *sitting a few rows further back.* JULES *tries to attract* JIM's *attention.* CATHERINE *throws a ball of paper at him. Finally* JIM *turns round, sees* JULES *and* CATHERINE, *leaves his seat and goes back towards them. The three of them leave the auditorium together. We see them again passing through the foyer of the cinema. Lovingly,* JULES *arranges* CATHERINE's *scarf for her. She pauses for a moment and looks pensively at* JIM. *(Still on page 103) The three of them walk towards the car.*

VOICE *off*: Jim was glad to see Jules again, and to find that his heart no longer leapt on seeing Catherine. On her side, she avoided their being alone together and suggested that they went for a drive. Jim agreed.

> *We see the car again travelling very fast along a country road, zig-zagging from side to side.*

VOICE *off*: What was in store for them this time? . . . Catherine drove fast and slightly dangerously. There was an atmosphere of expectation, as there had been during the drive through the forest before their meeting with Albert. They stopped at an open-air café beside the river.

Shot of the three of them seated at a table in the garden with drinks in front of them.

JULES : Now they're beginning to burn books.

JIM : Yes, it's unbelievable.

CATHERINE *gets up and leaves the table.* JULES *and* JIM *watch her for a moment without speaking.*

JULES : For Catherine, you were easy to get in the first place and difficult to keep. Your love fell to zero, then rose to a hundred again with that of Catherine. I have never known your zeros . . . nor your hundreds.

Reverse shot of CATHERINE *standing by the car.*

CATHERINE : *Monsieur* Jim, I have something to say to you. Will you come with me?

She gets into the car and sits at the wheel while JIM *gets up and joins her. The camera pans slowly after him, then more rapidly, coming to rest on* CATHERINE *who calls out to* JULES.

CATHERINE : Jules, watch us carefully.

Inside the car, CATHERINE *sits at the wheel and looks at* JIM *and smiles at him very tenderly.* JULES *watches the car from the table as it moves along the river bank. Long shot of the car as it starts to cross a bridge over the river. The bridge is in ruins and the middle arch is missing. (Still on page 104) At this moment,* JULES, *realising the danger or suddenly waking up to the reality of what is happening, gets up in alarm. The next shot is taken through the windscreen of the car, as it approaches the gap in the bridge. Close-up of* CATHERINE, *concentrating hard, yet looking almost ironic.*

Then we see, shot from below, the car shooting off the edge of the bridge, turning over and over. It hits the water and disappears, leaving a few ripples on the surface.

VOICE *off* : No longer would Jules suffer from the fear he had had from the very beginning, first that Catherine would be

99

unfaithful to him, and then only that she might die . . . for now it had happened.

A shot of reeds in the water dissolves to the interior of a crematorium.

Four pall-bearers pass across the screen bearing a coffin and put it down beside another one. JULES *enters the building behind them.*

VOICE *off* : They found the bodies entangled in the reeds. Jim's coffin was unnaturally large, Catherine's a mere casket by comparison. They left nothing behind them. Jules had his daughter. Had Catherine liked struggling for the sake of the struggle? No. But she had sown chaos in Jules's life until he was sick of it. *Close-up of* JULES. A feeling of relief swept over him. His friendship with Jim had no equivalent in love. Together they found amusement and satisfaction in mere trifles; the discovery of their differences did not lessen their affection. From the very beginning of their friendship, they had been called Don Quixote and Sancho Panza.

Long shot of the inside of the crematorium. JULES *steps to one side and, in close-up, anonymous hands uncover the coffins and push each of them into an oven. Doors close behind each coffin. Dissolve to the hands opening the double doors of the ovens . . . then dissolve again to the ashes and charred remains which are ground up and put into small urns.*

Cut to a cemetery, in the daytime. Preceded by two attendants, each carrying an urn, JULES *crosses the cemetery and approaches the columbarium. (Still on page 104)*

VOICE *off* : The ashes were collected in urns and put into a pigeon-hole which was then sealed up. If he had been alone, Jules would have mixed them together. Catherine had always wished hers to be scattered to the winds from the top of a hill . . . but it was not allowed.

Once the urns have been sealed up in the pigeon-hole, JULES *goes down the steps from the columbarium and crosses the cemetery towards the exit. As he walks slowly away, the words* THE END *appear on the screen.*

100